ON POETRY

Glyn Maxwell

On Poetry

Harvard University Press
Cambridge, Massachusetts
2013

Copyright © Glyn Maxwell, 2012
Printed in the United States of America

First published in the United Kingdom by Oberon Books Ltd, London 2012

First Harvard University Press edition, 2013

Full acknowledgement for extracts reproduced in this book
can be found on pages 172-173.

'The Byelaws' by Glyn Maxwell was first published in *The Times
Literary Supplement* in 2012

Library of Congress Cataloging-in-Publication Data

Maxwell, Glyn, 1962–
On poetry / Glyn Maxwell. — First Harvard University Press edition.
pages   cm
ISBN 978-0-674-72566-9 (cloth : alk. paper)
1. Poetry.   2. English language—Versification.   3. English poetry—History
and criticism.   4. American poetry—History and criticism.   I. Title.
PR6063.A869O52   2013
808.1—dc23   2013017169

for Mara Jebsen, Charlotte Walker,
Jesse Ball and Arthur Moffa

Contents

'Oh, then I must be going, child!' said Meet-on-the-Road.
'So fare you well, so fare you well,' said Child-as-it-Stood.

Anon

White

T HIS IS A book for anyone.

There are as many outlooks on poetry, on poets, on poems, on poetics, as there are people who read, but my book is for anyone. So forgive me if I leap as far back in time as possible to find a place where we all agree.

*

This far: alert, curious, more or less naked, without language, looking out over the green savannah. Now that was a leap, that's an outlook. You see an open space with trees whose branches spread out near the ground and bear fruit. You see a river or path that winds away out of sight, beyond the horizon. You see a few animals, you see changing clouds. You like what you see. Two hundred thousand years later you'll call this outlook 'beautiful' but the word's no use to you now.

Time after time, in the field of evolutionary psychology, the children of today, from anywhere on earth, in test conditions, point to this picture, choose it over all others – forests, jungles, mountains, beaches, deserts – as the view most pleasing to them. What are they looking at? What are they *really* looking at?

Well, evolutionary psychologists think they're looking at this: an open space (we can hunt) with trees (we can hide) whose branches spread out near the ground (we can escape) and bear fruit (we can eat). We see a river (we can drink, wash, eat) or path (we can travel) that winds away out of sight (we can learn), beyond the horizon (we can imagine). We see a few animals (we can eat more), we see changing clouds (rains will come again, we can tell one day from another) and, all in all, we like what we see. What evolutionary psychologists – and I – believe is that aesthetic preferences, those things we find beautiful, originate not in what renders life delightful or even endurable, but in what makes life *possible*.

*

Art, drawing, writing, poetry – are marks made in time by that gazing creature. Poetry has been unnecessary for almost all of creation. Strictly speaking it still is. But it happens to be my savannah, this *strictly speaking*, and it may well be yours, so let's advance together, alert, curious, naked – or at least two of those – into our first landscape, admiring once again what we can't be without.

*

And, since this is a writer's book about writing, let's stop to take with us a leaf from one of the earliest such books to have reached us, Aristotle's *Politics*, where the philosopher observes that 'practically everything has been discovered on many occasions...in the course of the ages; for necessity may be supposed to have taught men the inventions that were absolutely required, and, when these were provided, it was natural that other things which would adorn or enrich life should grow up by degrees.'

Let's start again with nothing. Let's start with poetry's inventions that are absolutely required – their names are *something* and *nothing* – and see what comes of them.

Imagine whiteness, a blank sheet of paper, the white screen...

Ready the black of ink or pixels or *you*...

Do this if only to remind yourself that the writing of a poem is a physical act, a deed that elbows into its space and time in the day or the night. The passing of the quill, the fountain-pen, the typewriter, the iPad – this too shall pass – never changed anything. Perhaps I'm addressing you whose need to write verse, to score lines into silence, to drum your fingers into the dark, rises in you in a tangible way, like a tonic, an act of self-healing, a way how not to feel inadequate, empty, forsaken, ill. These adjectives won't seem exaggerated to you I'm talking to. Put the blank paper, or the empty screen, right to one side there, and start to know it.

*

Regard the space, that ice plain, that dizzying light. That past, that future. Already it isn't nothing. At the very least it's your enemy, and that's an awful lot. Poets work with two materials, one's black and one's white. Call them sound and silence, life and death, hot and cold, love and loss: any can be the case but none of those yins and yangs tell the whole story. What you feel the whiteness *is right now* – consciously or more likely some way beneath that plane – will determine what you do next. Call it this and that, whatever it is *this time*, just don't make the mistake of thinking the white sheet is nothing. It's nothing for your novelist, your journalist, your blogger. For those folk it's a *tabula rasa*, a giving surface. For a poet it's half of everything. If you don't know how to use it you are writing prose. If you write poems that you might call free and I might call unpatterned then skilful, intelligent use of the whiteness is all you've got.

Put more practically, line-break is all you've got, and if you
don't *master* line-break – the border between poetry and prose
– then you don't know there is a border. And there is a border.
(A prose poem is prose done by a poet.) More of this later, let's
just keep staring out that whiteness, get accustomed to its face.

*

You want to hear the whiteness eating? Write out the lyrics of
a song you love. Twenty years or so back I might have pointed
out that the generations of young poets who judged rhyme a
thing of the past nevertheless knew off by heart a good two
hundred rock lyrics knitted as gaily as Mother Goose. Maybe
some quality rap songs made the old cat-sat-mat thing conscious
again. But do write something down. Rock, rap, folk, show-
tune, anything, but something written for music, something
regarded as truly wonderful in its world, loved by you, loved by
your world. Let it try breathing in the whiteness I'm speaking of.

Anything you like. I mean love. Say mine is Dylan's late song
'Not Dark Yet'. I think that's a timeless song, as memorable as
Robert Frost – but, unlike Frost, it shrinks in the whiteness.
Written down it looks amateurish, Hallmark. Try it with the
best, really. Cole Porter, Rodgers & Hammerstein, John and
Paul, Leonard Cohen, Joni Mitchell, Bob Marley, Tom Waits,
Tori Amos, Eminem, Jay-Z, try it. If you strip the music off it
it dies in the whiteness, can't breathe there. Without the music
there is nothing to mark time, to *act* for time.

Song lyrics are not written upon whiteness, so the whiteness
is alien to them, a corroding air, you can *hear* it eating those
sweet lines away. Song lyrics are not composed to take the form

of black signs *upon* that whiteness, therefore the blackness itself is alien, doesn't have the blood the sung words have.

I give to you and you give to me true love, true love. Yesterday all my troubles seemed so far away. How does it feel to be on your own? Let's get together and feel alright. Do you remember when we used to sing Sha la la, la la, la la, la la, l-la te da?

This feels like wanton cruelty to most beautiful birds, but when you force a creature from its element it dies before you. Nothing's true anymore, what you have is a bad translation. If you don't agree, you're still clouding the thing with the music you love. If you turn it down to silence and still think you're looking at poetry, you and I can't go any further. You should probably form a band.

*

The other half of everything for the songwriters is music. For the poets it's silence, the space, the whiteness. Music for them – and silence for us – *does the work of time.* I think our gig is harder. Their enemy reaches out, plays chords, goes hey we could be friends if you play your cards right. Our enemy simply waits, like it knows the arts of war. Songs are strung upon sounds, poems upon silence. Songwriters stir up a living tradition, poets make flowers grow in air. Bob Dylan and John Keats are at different work. It would be nice never to be asked about this again.

*

For let's remind ourselves how singular poetry is – I mean poetry that's primarily written to be read. The reader's role in this art-form is like nothing else, owing to the medium of poetry's creation, and to its relationship with time. In most encounters with art, time is entirely in the hands of the maker, the creator, the composer, the player: this is certainly true for a piece of music, theatre, dance, film, television, and equally so in the rough-edged versions of these – live music, improv, stand-up, performance poetry. So far, so obvious. Only in the visual arts – painting, sculpture, static installation – does the relationship change. Here the experience is not linear: one can encompass things in one's 'own time'. A poem on a page is linear, or suggests linearity without compelling it, but time remains one's own – or, more exactly, *voice upon time* does.

I always have to remind myself to spell it time not Time. When I say or hear or read or write the word that T towers over me always. The Christian won't go without his C, or his G. For He is never without his H. But in all cases we are honouring the *other*, the element in which we thrive and fail, the entity we've tried in a thousand ways to render *human* so it can hear our words. Time can be implacable Jahweh or merciful Jesus, but it's present to me like those creatures are present. Perhaps all poets are stricken into life by such a presence.

Poets are voices upon time. What makes poetry so giddyingly different from other forms is how naturally and plainly its reader can inhabit that voice. For we all consciously know that poetry is written in the everyday material of language, but at a deeper cerebral level surely it becomes easier to imagine the voice one's own, that *we* could be thinking it, living it, saying it. *We could have come to just this place.* How else could a great poem last so vertiginously long?

And because our inner voice dictates the texture, tone and timing of the reading that we both render and receive, the silence around it and throughout it seems to become ours too. We place it and hear it where we will. We characterise it *as* we will. A memorised poem can be passed to you intact. I think this makes the written poem unique, in terms of our relationship with its materials – by which I mean the black (something there) and the white (nothing there). The Stalin regime could destroy Osip Mandelstam, but not the poems his widow Nadezhda had learned by heart. That's something and nothing showing their true colours.

*

Start where we all remember. Pass some time in the great white spaces. What is the nature of the whiteness preceding the line below? Close your eyes, let's call it a silence this time, one of its other guises. Pretend no one ever thought of this line that's coming, pretend you think of it! If you don't like games like this you really shouldn't have come this far. Maybe you're too old for exclamation marks. Ha! Close your eyes. Wait... nothing... no... something...

Shall I compare thee to a summer's day?

Remember the quality of the space before. Poetry is an act, and I'm saying be an actor for a while. Wasn't it warm, sunlit, infused with joy and serenity, that crimson space the words came out of? Sounds like enough to me, a silence one can live with, no need to dip the nib in the bottle, not a time to be choosing fonts. But there is a need, for it's not enough. The black signs say it's not enough, because Shakespeare has something even better than how lovely it is and that's, at this moment, once, upon a time, to *say so*.

This exercise works best if, having pretended to think of the line, you actually write it down. Feel the power of the line you thought of – passing through you – into the pen, into the keys. Again, pretend you thought of it and look, now it's in your handwriting, or the font you named it in. But this happened to someone once, in our country, with hedgerows in the distance and a sparrow wittering on. Bear in mind again the actual time and space poetry claws from us, as you see those words appear. This deed should start to suggest to you also – and it's the slowing down that allows this – the unearthly weirdness of what you're doing. What on earth *are* you doing? This is where white goes black, where person becomes poem, where the ears of time prick up – *It* knows battle's been rejoined. Your love for the Beloved is now a series of preposterous black squiggles that will truly melt into nonsense if you stare at them too long. This is how you love? With these – *doodles*?

*

Let's go to the mountain, let's do as Shakespeare does, let's do some comparing, with spin-a-stick famous first lines from the 17th, 18th and 19th centuries. Let's imagine some moments of conception. Like he says elsewhere, nothing will come of nothing.

The lines below are approaching you. Generate a silence whose ending you're aware of, play the game again, imagine the quality of that ancient hush, make it yours and now, until, all of a sudden, as if from a blue sky –

> Had we but world enough, and time,
> This coyness, lady, were no crime...

This is the opening of Andrew Marvell's 'To His Coy Mistress', a plea for sex got up in its Sunday best as a hymn to love. Where the Shakespearean silence is a brimming over of thoughtful joy, vaguely post- as well as pre-coital, the Marvellian one is an unsated thirst, a need that spills out as rhythmic language, a lust so richly felt it tries at first to tickle – 'I by the tide/Of Humber would complain' and at last to terrify – 'worms shall try/That long preserved virginity' – the sweetheart into bed.

The poem's most famous lines will help us to hear the whiteness. After twenty lines of winningly ludicrous flattery – 'An hundred years should go to praise/Thine eyes, and on thy forehead gaze;/Two hundred to adore each breast' and so on and so forth – this happens:

> But at my back I always hear
> Time's wingéd chariot hurrying near
> And yonder all before us lie
> Deserts of vast eternity.

What is the cost of silence to this poem? What's the price of stopping there? It's to hear what he can hear: time passing, winged, *hurrying,* to make a desert of him and her and you and everyone. Now that is one annihilating whiteness. Want to hear how fast time moves? Not with the regular step of, say, 'The wingéd feet of Time draw near' – no, the word slams hard to the top of the line: '*Time's* wingéd chariot hurrying near...' You want to talk about iambs and dactyls and stress and unstress, as if the English language were some binary read-out, then you are missing the big picture.

You master form you master time.

The poem ends, the plea for *everything she is* ends, but the silence that follows doesn't sound like the howling wind it rides throughout, it sounds more like the rustle of silk in privacy, the hope spun into likelihood. It's no longer a plea to her, it's kind of a plan they've made.

> Thus, though we cannot make our sun
> Stand still, yet we will make him run.

*

You master form you master time. Well, you don't, but you give it a run for its non-exchangeable money. Form has a direct effect on the silence beneath it, which is to say on the whiteness before and after it and where the lines end. If you have lived a quarter-century and decided, because someone paid to teach you has told you, or because you read it somewhere, that form should be gone from poetry – meter, say, or rhyme, or regularity or pattern of any kind – then you are effectively saying that time is different these days. It's not what it was. Maybe you think time has been broken. Maybe you think it's been broken into fragments you can leap around or hide behind. Let's see you.

You're still here: play the game again. Skip the 18th century for a moment – time's so feeble, it won't defend itself – close your eyes, compose this one:

> There's a certain Slant of light,
> Winter Afternoons –

Could that silence be any different from the two we've just examined? No one else is there. In the world of her poems no one else ever seems to be there with Emily Dickinson, and yet she always seems to have just come back to her desk from her little bed and lit a candle, having seen the whole of Creation.

But here, no one is there. I do expect that both Shakespeare's and Marvell's poems were actually *written* alone, but the world they make – in an instant – encompasses a lady right there listening, with admirable patience, outdoors or in. Dickinson's world is one lone face in a window, a world seen whole, but from shelter. A 'Slant of light' is light indoors, refracted, dusty and filtered: there's the space established. The plural – not 'On a Winter Afternoon' but 'Winter Afternoons' – gives us the sense of long observation of the same thing from the same vantage: there's the time and tone set, the colour and picture made. The concision. You master form you master time. And yes, you don't, no one does, but that poem isn't going away, we're looking at poems that show no sign of leaving. Emily is still coming back to her desk from her bed and lighting a candle.

With the best poets you can play an archaeological game. Take a volume of the work, mist your eyes so you can't read a word, flutter through the pages, get a sense of the forms the poems take. Dickinson's are slight and skeletal against the white, like the bones of birds, stanzaic poems of John Donne or Thomas Hardy seem like worked gemstones with patterned edges. Whitman's line-ends seem like the wild blown edges of a ragged garment. This is the place to begin, peering at shapes. Assess the balance of the black creature and the white silence. Consider always what in this case the creature *is*, what in this case the silence *is*. And if they are *those* things, what pressures do they exert upon one another? To say the very least: a Christian and an atheist are dealing with considerably different creatures and silences. But so are the lover, the philosopher, the malcontent, the madman.

*

The next example, again, sits at a planetary distance from those before. This one has always struck me as the essence of poetry, the distillation. We'll come to it again when I'm done with the whiteness, we'll look instead at its blackness, but, meanwhile, the game again: stand in a world in which Samuel Coleridge hasn't written 'The Rime of the Ancient Mariner', hear the atmosphere before it, stumble on it, be seared by it, let it out –

> It is an ancient Mariner
> And he stoppeth one of three...

This is the beating of giant wings, the sound of the story that has to be told. It arrives with the day-lit suddenness of a ghost, unheralded, unwarned-of, and with truly frightening inhuman speed its – 'It is' not 'He is', 'It *is*' not 'It was' – *Its* hand is on your arm. *Its* hand is on *your* arm! It just stopped one of three: hope you're not the one. Three men are on their way to a wedding-banquet, can't wait to get stuck into the huge old pies and the porter or sack or maypole dance or whatever, you 'canst hear the merry din' – but without warning this happens. Not to all three, to *one*. And now the poem is happening, not to everyone, just to *you*.

Time could not go on as it was. The story has changed everything. What you could hear in the silence that preceded the voice was the irrepressible boiling-up of a raging need to *tell*. By the far end of the Mariner's tale, that odyssey of hell and high water – where the white space is now ocean, now desert, and the black figures now cursed, now blessed – the wedding-feast is over, the merriment foregone, the garden dark again, and the Mariner speaks for the unassuagable thirst of all the storytellers, all the poets:

> Since then, at an uncertain hour,
> That agony returns:
> And till my ghastly tale is told,
> This heart within me burns.

*

Now of course we are commandeering time to play like this: retrospectively characterising spaces that, in purely scientific terms, look identical and surely cannot possess character. But time refracts oddly in the vicinity of verse, as anyone who writes it knows already. In any case, to say poetic thought isn't a science cuts both ways. As well as scorning poetry for being too vague and amorphous to define by law or principle, one may amiably retort that scientific method proves inadequate in the face of it. We know by experience that language itself is inadequate. You can't find better words for the best words. Just for this sense of whiteness – before we even have a word on our page – we need nine thousand names for white and we have one. These silences are different. What grew in them was different. If it's obvious that the fibre of the black determines the cloth of the white, it needs to be remembered that the reverse is true too.

Imagine the negative of a poem on a page, white script on black. You're blundering through arctic night with your little lantern swinging. Think of poetry cold and dark like that: what will it need *at least*? A heart, a heartbeat, warmth, a place to go.

*

The point of the game we play is to remind us that a poem, any poem, however old or venerable or indestructible it seems, arises from the urge of a human creature, *once, upon a time* – to break silence, fill emptiness, colour nothing with something, anything. That the above examples suggest so much, give us so many dimensions in so little space, is merely testament to the power of those poets. The principle is the same. It doesn't help to bend the knee before concepts of *inspiration* – unless you remember that word's etymology of the breath. Then it helps, because if some Techie Enchanter long before his time had made audio recordings of the composition of these poems, the scratchy silence would be peppered with sharp intakes of *breath*.

Talking of scratches, if you want to hear silence and sound and past and future meet at a memorable crossroads, have a listen to Alfred, Lord Tennyson in 1890, recording 'The Charge of the Light Brigade' onto a wax cylinder provided for him by a Mr Edison, the very man, that true Techie Enchanter ahead of his time. Or, in the first ever audio capture of poetry, Robert Browning at a dinner party a year before, attempting his 'How They Brought the Good News from Ghent to Aix' for some assembly of thoroughly bearded gentlemen. It goes like this.

> I sprang to the saddle, and Joris, and he,
> I galloped, Dirck galloped, we galloped all three,
> 'Speed' echoed the wall to us galloping through,
> 'Speed' echoed the...
> Then the gate shut behind us, the lights sank to rest...

I'm terribly sorry but I can't remember me own verses, but one thing I shall remember all me life is this astonishing… *[unclear]…*by your wonderful invention! Robert Browning! Bravo bravo bravo! Hip, hip, hooray! Hip, hip, hooray! Hip, hip, hooray! Bravo!

I love how he shouts his own name. Perhaps he thought for a second of dismay the future was sending its only lifeboat.

Poets were real, walked around, sat down, shouted. Poems are responses to needs, urges, hungers, thirsts, they have sprouted forth in moments like the moments we know, passing beside us now, five-to-nine in the morning, four-twenty in the day, indoors, outdoors, sun and rain, with a king on the throne, with a fool or a child or no one. They get worked on, worked at, thrown out, messed with, but there is a moment, we all know there's a moment in which the poem (the black signs on white surfaces) takes over from the self, becomes the self for now. I spend my allotted slice of forever contemplating that moment.

Of course, if you devote yourself to the life, them black signs on white surfaces are, by and by, *all you'll be*, so you might as well get used to them. If you really stick with this you will end up jealous of your own words. You'll be your own ghost reading them, secretly delighted, secretly aghast. In your old age the Devil will point at your piled-up volumes of poetry and say *There, I made you immortal like I promised*, and you'll croak from the white sheets *Damn the work, I meant Me, I meant Me!* and the Devil will say *I know! Ha! Too old for exclamation marks, eh!* And be gone.

But think once more of the white turning to black, of the nib putting down on the paper, or the pixels going dark because of whatever gazillion signals you just cluelessly set in order – think of where person becomes poem. What do you want to send through that portal? Should it not sound like you, act like you, breathe like you? Or at the very least like a human?

What *is* the poem if it doesn't sound, act, think, breathe, like a human? What does it know? What can it tell? What are we to it, what is it to us? What could it ever be to us? Because where else could it have come from?

*

Back again with the whiteness. You have to see the whole of a poem to appreciate the field it's growing in, so here, in white and black, is the whole of a poem. Contemplate the before, the world without this poem, then pretend you suddenly rapidly write it in some elongated narcotic swoon – this is meant to be fun sometimes – but be keenly aware of, or if you like druggily focused on, the white spaces between the stanzas, be clear what they are. This, W. B. Yeats's 'The Song of Wandering Aengus', is the simplest and most beautiful illustration I can think of. Write it. Feel the urge to tell it, feel the air, the weather, the season, try to sound out the silence below it all. This poem has never been written. Write it. Be writing it. Have written it.

> I went out to the hazel wood,
> Because a fire was in my head,
> And cut and peeled a hazel wand,
> And hooked a berry to a thread;
> And when white moths were on the wing,
> And moth-like stars were flickering out,
> I dropped the berry in a stream
> And caught a little silver trout.

When I had laid it on the floor
I went to blow the fire aflame,
But something rustled on the floor,
And some one called me by my name:
It had become a glimmering girl
With apple blossom in her hair
Who called me by my name and ran
And faded through the brightening air.

Though I am old with wandering
Through hollow lands and hilly lands,
I will find out where she has gone,
And kiss her lips and take her hands;
And walk among long dappled grass,
And pluck till time and times are done
The silver apples of the moon,
The golden apples of the sun.

Three stanzas, two spaces between them, not to mention the mists at either end. *Stanza* is the Italian word for – look it up. Maybe you have Google close at hand (capital G like God) or even a *reference-book* in some other room? The attic, try. Find the room with the answer.

What's in these two spaces? What could be simpler? A change of place, a passing of time. The 'little silver trout' dangles from the rod over the river, dangles across the void into the next stanza. In the void the poet went away from the stream with his precious catch, out of the hazel wood and home. Now the little silver trout is on his floor by the fire. If you look closely at the line 'When I had laid it on the floor' you can tell the fish is not alive. There are verbs that could have let it wriggle a little. This only matters because it's about to turn into a Vision and change the poet's world. But we're still with the whiteness. The next one is heartbreaking. Here it is again, the stanza-break:

> And faded through the brightening air.

> Though I am old with wandering

Hear that? *See* that? All a man's youth and adulthood went by there, streamed through in that centimetre, that white torrent. In song it goes that way. What Yeats calls a 'Song' is only a 'song' for me because it floats down and bobs so very truly on the air, like all his early poems, 'Down By the Salley Gardens', 'When You Are Old', 'He Wishes For the Cloths of Heaven'…

It's a poem, though, let's get that straight. If you're still missing your favourite tunes, you might reflect, in the company of two great Irishmen, upon how Van Morrison's 'Brown-Eyed Girl' is *essentially* the same sweet mystery as this poem: though the Yeats is otherworldly and the Morrison earthbound, still, love in youth is gazed back at by a man in age, and the imprint left is a sorrow that shines. Well, many songs do this more or less, but let's dwell only on the best of them.

*

An exercise that is useful and fun to do with any great poem is to write its screenplay. Here's how to understand the whiteness. This way you can see how some stanza-breaks are cuts, some are fades, some are dissolves. I think the 'silver trout' one is a cut and the 'brightening air' one a dissolve to white and out again. These aren't yes-or-no questions, the value is entirely in the contemplation and the fun in the guessing, but what must be exact to the screenwriter can be revelatory to the poet. If in the great family of the writing arts Poetry is the hard-up eldest son and Screenplay the little bro who's loaded, nonetheless these two are close, enjoy each other's company, they share longer walks than either shares with Playwriting or Fiction, all the difficult middle children. You have to have tried all of these arts to make hay with the metaphor, to have found this out. In time, if you want to learn about any of them, try your hand at them all. Just as an exercise, run the same little fictional *event* through all of them: turn a sonnet to a film to a story to a scene. See what changes in the telling, what comes to it, what falls away.

Or you could do this with your whole writing life. No one will ever know who you are, and you will never need to tell them.

*

Take nine sheets of blank paper and pretend the following things about them:

That the first page is physically hurt by your every word.

That the second page is *turned on* by every syllable.

That every mark on the third page makes you *remember more.* On the fourth, less, like dementia.

That God can only hear you if you're writing on the fifth page.

That only touching the sixth page are you hidden from God.

That every word you write on the seventh prolongs the time from now until the moment you meet that mythical creature known as The One.

That every word you write on the eighth brings that moment closer, yes, but makes your time together shorter.

The ninth page says you have *only nine words left in your life.*

The nine sheets are nine battlefields. The black will win some, the white will win some, it will be silly as war and bloody as chess. If you get any poems out of it, any lines at all, pin them to your breast. If you get any white sheets, bury them with honours. Remember where you won, remember where you lost. Wonder why.

~

Black

IN MY WORK the white is everything but me, and the black is me. In poems the black is someone. In every poem I admire, and every poem that's still around say fifty, a hundred, a thousand years after its maker is gone, what's signalled by the black shapes is a human presence. An illusion of a human presence, granted, but let's swallow that and move on. I mean, I'm not sitting next to you.

All I believe, and therefore all I teach – which is why I don't need a book any longer than this, though I could talk a *very* long night on the placing of 'the' – is that the form and tone and pitch of any poem should coherently express the presence of a human creature. Content, matter, subject, these all play little part. Form plays almost every part, which is why I continue to say that who masters form masters time. I continue then to concede that nothing masters time as in the-deity-I-go-by – it's a deity, so I believe both that it can hear me and that it needs placating – but a poet can shape time in a poem, and form is how that's done. So words like 'formalist' or 'formalism' mean very little to me. These categories make for nonsense. I was once branded a 'neo-con' by some online shadow, as if my work with rhyme and meter made me hawkish and pro-torture. I visualised some Dante-deep ring of cyberspace where only shit is spoken.

*

Then again Dante Alighieri was there already, he met Nimrod there, the architect of Babel, the founder of confusion, between the Eighth and Ninth Circles of the Inferno he met him:

Raphel mai ameche zabi almi!

bellowed the giant in a nonsense-tongue Dante dreamed up. It translates into nothing at all.

*

I imagine it is possible to write a poem that does not coherently express the presence of a human creature, but I don't believe such a thing could survive time better than its maker. Paper versus fire, or, as Delmore Schwartz has it, 'Time is the school in which we learn,/Time is the fire in which we burn.' The harder certain poets might try to absent the human presence from a poem, and many do on perfectly valid experimental grounds – and all experiment is valid – the more obviously the human presence stands there, in a clever disguise, doing just that. I come home from such poems still feeling I met someone on the road, only they were wearing a clever disguise, so out of kindness I pretended not to know them. In such a case, intentionally or no, the human presence looms very large indeed.

A poem in a mask can be wonderful. A poem that keeps putting it on and taking it off again *could* be wonderful, I'm open to everything, but what matters is why. *Why* would you do that? I've seen who you are now. I think a poem you read has to meet the same criteria as a person you meet: did it mean anything to you, matter to you, affect you? If it didn't do those things you won't remember it long. Think of ourselves before language again, hiding or hunting somewhere on that lonely bright savannah – you have to remember a thing to know about it, so others can be shown. You have to remember a thing to learn from it, so others can be told. You have to remember a thing to care about it, so life can be borne easier.

*

Here's someone you do remember.

> It is an ancient Mariner
> And he stoppeth one of three.
> 'By thy long grey beard and glittering eye,
> Now wherefore stopp'st thou me?
>
> The bridegroom's doors are opened wide,
> And I am next of kin;
> The guests are met, the feast is set:
> Mayst hear the merry din.'
>
> He holds him with his skinny hand,
> 'There was a ship,' quoth he.
> 'Hold off! unhand me, grey-beard loon!'
> Eftsoons his hand dropped he.
>
> He holds him with his glittering eye –
> The Wedding-Guest stood still,
> And listens like a three years' child:
> The Mariner hath his will.

The Wedding-Guest will be gone a while, he has a long poem to hear. But imagine you are one of the other two. You're a wedding-guest, but you're not 'The Wedding-Guest'. You're one of his two friends, we'll call them Ned Stowey and Bill Porlock. You fellows press on to the wedding-feast, you don't wait to hear the story. You will never hear the rhymes of the ancient mariner, let alone read 'The Rime of the Ancient Mariner'. Not now, not soon, not *eftsoons*. You still met him, though. He wanted a *Word*. You had an encounter with *a Word*.

*

It happened in the moment. A weird old boy halted your friend and started talking at him. It made no sense at the time so you moved on to the bar. In the final chapter of this book I'll tell you what I think happened next to Mr Stowey and Mr Porlock, but let us focus on their brief encounter with the Mariner...

1. Weird old boy, made no sense, moved on to the bar. Whatever happened in the moment, let's think of it as the daylit way of meeting, the daylit way of meaning. We'll call it *solar*.

2. Now there's what the moment meant to you, how a word comes back in memory or dream or a sleepless night or a poem – *What ship? Who was that weird old boy? Why did he do that?* Let's think of this as the moonlit way of meeting or meaning, the resonance, the echo, the *lunar*.

3. There was his voice at the time. 'There was a ship.' A seafarer's voice, Cornish say, central casting. There's the sound of the word. Call that *musical*.

4. There was his face at the time. Grey beard, glittering eye, wild, make-up department... There was the look of the word. *Visual*.

32

Solar, lunar, musical, visual. Four ways of meeting, four ways of meaning. Real-life meeting can add to that three other senses – smell, taste, feeling – and all we synaesthetic oddballs who write poetry know full well that words can do all three of them for us – smell, taste and feel like things – but let's calm the excitable metaphor down: it's our servant, after all.

Having said that, when I once cheerfully asked a graduate class to confirm that the word 'someone' is indeed, as I had known since childhood, red in colour, that the word 'everyone' is blue-grey, and the word 'anyone' pale yellow, every student came up with his or her completely different colours. It didn't seem fair to fail them on that basis, though I was tempted.

I'd certainly have failed Arthur Rimbaud for writing that poem called 'Voyelles' in which he calls 'A noir, E blanc, I rouge, U vert, O bleu'. Amateur. *Anyone* knows it's A yellow, E blue, I white, O black, U purple. What do you think it is? Please don't say. Maybe synaesthesia is something one does alone.

*

A word and four ways. Prime meaning, resonant meanings, way it *sounds* sans meaning, way it *looks* sans meaning. Solar, lunar, musical, visual. I think the best poems encompass all four, in such a way that your meeting with a poem is like your meeting with a person. The more like that it is, the better the poem is, the longer you remember it, the longer it lasts, the 'sadder' and 'wiser' a wedding-guest you'll be when you rise on the morrow morn. The better life will be for it.

Think of meetings in which any one of these four is weak. If little passed between you in the solar moment, there'll be little coming at you in the lunar time. Though if in fact it turns out that you just met your future life-partner yet you *still* think little passed between you, then the lunar presence – dream, daydream, art and so on – will softly and irrevocably set you right. It will also prove that the face and voice which you hazily remember made in truth a dizzying impression. If little passed between you, and little is remembered, and the voice has faded, and the face has blurred – if any one of these is true – then your meeting was insignificant, the poem inadequate. Or, in your encounter with person or poem, perhaps *you* were. To uphold the metaphor, it does rather take two.

*

1. Poems deficient in solar meaning are quite easy to spot in the field, because vast trapezoids of critical scaffold have been constructed around them to clank in the wind. Measuring devices have been set up to record all resonance real and imagined. Cults spring up in the meadows thereabouts; outsiders are unwelcome. The Hard Question: *what actually happened here and is there a good enough reason why NOT SAYING held sway over SAYING?* No major poet has been used as a smokescreen for obscurity more than Ezra Pound, yet it's he who writes: 'Language is the main means of human communication. If an animal's nervous system does not transmit sensations and stimuli, the animal atrophies.' He also wrote, and I quote, for intemperate lovers of metaphor everywhere: 'the natural object is always the adequate symbol.' Get it in the sunlight.

2. Poems deficient in lunar meaning... They might have immediate impact, might be strong on comedy, misery, shock-value, perhaps impressive in live performance.

But written down the words are flat, go nowhere else, are awaiting instructions from their leader. The Hard Question: *can I take it home from here?* (All song lyrics written down or recited are in this category, if only because the absent music plays the lunar role.)

3. Poems weak in music. They sound like prose, are dull to read and hard to memorise. Try. Because they sound like prose the mind relaxes: nothing urgent here, nothing to fear, nothing to learn. Bright areas of the brain go dark. Poems deaf to the emotional work of vowels and the storyboarding of consonants. The Hard Question: *is this worth the candle?* On the bright side – poems *primarily* strong in music: beautiful nonsense verse like 'Jabberwocky' and 'The Dong with the Luminous Nose', or the utterances of spirits both benign: 'Where the bee sucks, there suck I...' and otherwise: 'Double, double toil and trouble...' Where kids should start. Pound again: 'Music rots when it gets *too far* from the dance. Poetry atrophies when it gets too far from music.'

4. Poems without a visual intelligence. From someone blind to the whiteness. Weak on line-break, weak on the causes of line-break. A beginner will say 'this is just broken-up prose' because you know what, there ain't nothing wrong with the eyes of a beginner. The Hard Question: *if you don't know what you're up to, why should I trust you?* On the bright side – poems with prime visual force: anything that's using *letter*-shape, *word*-shape, *line*-shape, *stanza*-shape or *poem*-shape as metaphor in itself. This can range from the use of 'I' and 'O' as the only pictograms we have in English

– a lonely figure, a cry of woe – to the 'O' as sun or moon, or the double 'oo' as eyes, as in Auden's lines 'Nor sorrow take/His endless look'. A child's eyes still quite intact: a profound alertness to what shapes remind you of other shapes. At the far end of this: 'concrete' poetry, George Herbert's 'Easter Wings' which is shaped like wings; Christian poems in the shape of the Cross; the tale told by a mouse to Alice in Wonderland. 'Mine is a long and a sad tale', says the mouse, which Alice mistakes for 'tail' so that it looks like a tail on the page, at which point she reasons: 'It's a long tail, certainly, but why do you call it sad?' A memorable example at the stanzaic level: Thomas Hardy's lines on the loss of the *Titanic*:

> In a solitude of the sea,
> Deep from human vanity,
> And the Pride of Life that planned her, stilly couches she.

> Steel chambers, late the pyres
> Of her salamandrine fires,
> Cold currents thrid, and turn to rhythmic tidal lyres.

> Over the mirrors meant
> To glass the opulent
> The sea-worm crawls – grotesque, slimed, dumb, indifferent...

Switch the black and white around: ocean liners in the middle of nowhere.

*

Work that has lasted is alert to all four of these ways of meaning. Translators, by the way, have at the outset to contemplate the loss of *all four* in transit, and must find equivalence for each one in the mother-tongue, must take them in like orphaned siblings. Make the poem bright at the reading, true in the echo, strong to the ear, right by the eye. An English translator has to make an English poet of his foreign friend, or he's just telling you some great dream he had.

*

A poem coherently expresses the presence of a human creature. By which I mean the same creature, in a consistent relation to you. For example, standing a few feet away in a field, saying aloud into the wind: 'Something there is that doesn't love a wall...' Intoning from a high lectern to the rafters of a hall: 'Do not go gentle into that good night...' Muttering next to you, mid-afternoon in a sad pub, having drained a generous G-and-T: 'They fuck you up, your mum and dad...' A *consistent relation.* The relation can change and still be consistent. The creature can approach you, back away from you, be gone a while, but this can only work if the relation changes like a human presence might change it. In the whiteness the poet can change it, make time pass, distance grow.

> The room was suddenly rich and the great bay-window was
> Suddenly spawning snow and pink roses against it
> Soundlessly collateral and incompatible:
> World is suddener than we fancy it.

In Louis MacNeice's 'Snow' witness the sheer force of the opening, that wide-open line-break, the terrible plenty as he sits forward in amazement gabbling the homely crackling old Anglo-Saxon 'room', 'great', 'window', 'snow', before settling into

37

multisyllabic Latinate 'collateral', 'incompatible', colourless in contrast, force lessening in the newer, exterior layers of English, as the impression turns from *light* to *thought*, then shrugs into the cheerful bar-room proverbial: 'World is suddener than we fancy it.' These are lines roaming the history of the language as the creaturely posture changes – where he's looking, how he's sitting, what he's doing – but it changes like we change.

Whether hunting or hiding on that green savannah, everything depends on relations of distance, so the next few examples relate to foreground and background. How much of your field of vision does the poet take? In the jumble of first lines below, which poet is saying *Look at me*? Which is saying *Don't look at me*? Both openings draw attention to the same thing: *me*. How present is the poet in these four cases? Which poet is saying *Look past me into the distance*? Which one *Look by me into the past*?

So to the Celestial Cocktail Party: you've scarcely sipped your free ambrosia served by sylphs and cherubs when four poets come at you from each of the four walls – 'Earth has not anything to show more fair...' 'Oh, talk not to me of a name great in story!' 'Well, they are gone, and here I must remain...' 'St Agnes' Eve – Ah, bitter chill it was!'

If this provides an impression of giddily changing foreground and background, silhouettes looming up and away again, fine. If this induces a migraine all the better. What a terrible poem they would make together. What a hideous sound is made when relations are neither consistent nor coherent. But take a step with each in turn, and see how a true meeting begins. Let

Wordsworth guide you to the open window, he wants to show you Westminster Bridge:

> Earth has not anything to show more fair:
> Dull would be he of soul who could pass by
> A sight so touching in its majesty...

Now Coleridge rudely interrupts, hustles you off to a corner so he can vent for a while. If you don't let him he might do the 'Mariner' again and that's your whole evening:

> Well, they are gone, and here I must remain,
> This lime-tree bower my prison! I have lost
> Beauties and feelings, such as would have been
> Most sweet to my remembrance...

A Cockney mutter in your ear – who let *him* in? – wants to tell you another story. Poor John Keats doesn't even want to be here and doesn't need you to see his face:

> St Agnes' Eve – Ah, bitter chill it was!
> The owl, for all his feathers, was a-cold...

And now who comes limping flamboyantly across the room to take you away from all this, tell you what he knows, worldly-wisdom everyone should have, his voice filling the room as he draws you towards the bar:

> Oh, talk not to me of a name great in story;
> The days of our youth are the days of our glory;
> And the myrtle and ivy of sweet two-and-twenty
> Are worth all your laurels though ever so plenty...

The name's Byron, Lord Byron. Not a bad party. The point is, these are four 'Romantics', poets consigned to a common name, and yet see how instantly four vastly separate, *coherent, consistent* presences draw you into faraway spheres.

*

Look at me. Don't look at me. Look by me into the past. Look past me into the distance.

Pick up a magazine of contemporary poetry and try to put into a sentence, as short as those above, *what is really being said* by the beginnings of poems. Deconstruct them. A brief glance at some recent work furnishes me with the following: Look at what I'm not doing. Look somewhere else. Look at you. Look at how I'm doing this (though I'm not doing this). Look at nothing. Regardez le mot *regardez*. Regardez le mot *mot*.

Any of these can work if they act upon you like a meeting with a human creature. I might not think them auspicious openings, I often don't, but it's what comes next that matters. In this way it is possible to be, in principle, open to anything at all.

Much contemporary verse is colloquial, prosaic, apparently 'free', going about its business without rhyme or meter or stanzaic pattern of any kind. But such poems, to survive, need two essential components: first their makers need to have truly mastered line-break, which is simply to say that he or she can keenly feel the pressure of silence; second, the poem must act upon you in a way that resembles a human encounter. For alone, in your memory, you, *you*, what's the difference – to the cells, to the synapses – between a poem you remember and a person you recall? You want lamps to go on.

*

Say that party really happened. The young man or woman – probably young lady, hemmed in by those four gents – goes home, assuming she extricated herself from Byron, she goes home intoxicated by these four meetings, intoxicated anyhow, throws open her window in hope of some kind of owl-song, or failing that some moonlight, let's call her Isabella, and she sets about writing her Best Poem Ever:

> How oft, at school, with most believing mind,
> (I speak of one from many singled out)
> I wander'd in a forest thoughtlessly
>   As sure as Heaven shall rescue me,
> I heard the sky-lark warbling in the sky,
>   By the light of the moon.

This won't look quite so good to Isabella in the cold light of dawn. Then again none of those lines are hers. It would have been better to have written in her diary: 'This bloke pointed out some old bridge he likes. A stoner told me how sad he was feeling. An emo boy had this random story. Finally this hot guy with a limp said hey life's like that and he knew of a better party.' Well she will keep going to book launches.

But it feels wrong to poke fun at one's own fantasy creatures, so we'll leave Isabella to sleep it off. She and her friends and many many many like them write poems like that every day and publish them every quarter. And when they don't make sense that's *how* they don't.

*

The younger arts can help us. As film helps with stanza-break, let photography help with first lines. Imagine any first line as a photographic *frame*. How much of the frame is taken up by the face of the poet? Is his or her *whole* figure in the poem, is he or she farther away? Back to you, gesturing into the distance? Hovering spectrally above? Seated, standing, walking? Is the picture in colour? What does he or she think of you? Can you be seen at all? Is the poet present at all? The last I can answer: yes, a blackness has marked the whiteness, someone is there. Consider *how* he or she is there, how the poet is imprinted on the poem. There is never no reason.

What's in the *frame* of each of these lines in this little cacophony?

Percy Bysshe Shelley: 'As I lay asleep in Italy...'

Alfred Edward Housman: 'They say my verse is sad: no wonder...'

Christina Rossetti: 'Does the road wind uphill all the way?'

Charlotte Mew: 'Up here, with June, the sycamore throws...'

Wilfred Owen: 'Down the close, darkening lanes they sang their way...'

What does 'I lay asleep' become in the light of 'in Italy'? Where are Housman's eyes looking – at us, beyond us, cast down? What does the *question* do to the view in Rossetti – does it blur the edges? Why is Mew 'with' June, not 'in' June? How does that alter the quality of the air? How many soldiers can you make out on Owen's 'lanes'? And how many more or fewer would you see if he'd written 'lane'?

*

Back on the savannah, how to survive? This survives because it is cunning (can't be caught) this survives because it is strong (can't be fought), this survives because it is lovely (must be saved). Three ways to be true. Poems survive because they are true. They can't do without craft or force. Beauty is a third essence. But all three are subsumed by truth. Here are the words of Keats's famous crockery: '"Beauty is truth, truth beauty," – that is all/Ye know on earth, and all ye need to know', or, as W. H. Auden has it, plainly and indestructibly, in 'Bucolics': 'nothing is lovely,/Not even in poetry, which is not the case.' It can't be beautiful if it isn't true.

Beauty, eh. Some are sure to find this a little bit *given*, lazily abstract, sentimental even. Then again, if some young poets were as watchful about needless obscurity as they are about needless sentimentality you might have heard of them.

But when I say *beauty* I don't mean the moon, or Isabella, or Isabella by moonlight. I mean one beholding anything or anybody as he or she did ages ago – I mean on our savannah – looking into the eyes of another, or at one's kindred say, or one's hunting-group, or out to the horizon, thinking *I can be safe here*, or *I will remember*, or *Life is finer than I know*. Beauty that evolved, was around us at times, beauty that made it, got here too, still trying to tell us where to hunt and hide and make love and make life.

*

Here's a very old poem, in about the oldest form there is, and it is very much 'the case'. I have the time, I light the candle, it's worth the candle. Whenever you read a poem it's your candle that's burning down, not the poet's. You've a finite stock of candles. This is a riddle, and the answer's not a candle, that's a red herring. And the answer's not a herring.

Wrætlic hongað   bi weres þeo,
frean under sceate.   Foran is þyrel.
Bið stiþ ond heard,   stede hafað godne;
þonne se esne   his agen hrægl
ofer cneo hefeð,   wile þæt cuþe hol
mid his hangellan   heafde gretan
þæt he efenlang ær   oft gefylde.

I've included the original as a by-the-by reminder that the black scribbles we know were once the black scribbles we once knew – or a handful of monks and scribes knew, at their workstations on the cutting edge, technological if not spiritual ancestors of the super-powered geeks you find there today. Only – stare at English words till the meanings drain away, and the new ones look as crazy as the old ones. That feels like a key to it all. And both monks and geeks a-chuckling at their desks would relish this riddle:

> *[Swings by his thigh a thing most magical!*
> *Below the belt, beneath the folds*
> *of his clothes it hangs, a hole in its front end,*
> *stiff-set and stout, it swivels about.*
> *Levelling the head of this hanging tool,*
> *its wielder hoists his hem above his knee;*
> *it is his will to fill a well-known hole*
> *that it fits fully when at full length*
> *he's oft filled it before. Now he fills it again.]*

Like I said, a key, bang on.

What kind of a meeting is this? Again, out of the mist, a figure looms ready to start on you instantly: a riddler. This is ancient fair exchange: you pay him attention and interest, he rewards you with winking double-entendre and clear-eyed revelation. Is it cunning, strong, lovely? Yes, it's still here. Above all it's true.

Might a poem so long-surviving be itself a key? It stops you like the Mariner, speaks entirely on its terms, goes away into the mist whence it came, leaving you changed a bit or a lot because you know something you didn't. You can proceed with your day, now you know what the Mariner went through. Now you know Westminster Bridge is lovely, that time's at your back in a winged chariot, that an old man finds grace in remembering a girl long-gone, that a key is in five or six ways sort of like a penis.

*

I say the riddler comes out of the mist. There are poems of mist and poems of smoke.

By mist I mean something natural that thins or parts or deepens further, something through which a shifting truth is glimpsed with joy, understanding – or spotted with fear. Mist: breathable, water going by in a cloak.

By smoke I mean man-made smoke, complex molecules conjured for reasons obscure, yet emanating from a single, explicable source. Clever to make, not clever to breathe. When you've blown it all away you're looking at a shell. By the time you get what it was you can't use it any more.

Roam the wide savannahs of the Tate Modern, breathe what's mist, smell what's smoke.

*

To conclude on the blackness and the whiteness we have to eavesdrop on one of my writing classes.

That's where Bella goes the next morning, having woken from a dream of meeting Wordsworth, Coleridge, Byron and Keats at a drinks party overlooking the Thames. *The river had a slope*, she tells Orlando when she meets him on the way. Orlando's parents joked with their dinner-party friends in the eighties about how, with a name like that, what a lover he would be some day! Well yes he is, Ollie's in love, he's besotted with Bella, but he doesn't know what to do with it. Bella says *Funny, why wasn't Shelley in my dream?* And Ollie quickens his step and says *er, maybe your subconscious dream-creator didn't have, you know, a copy of Shelley with her last night when she like, you know, created your dream* but he's gone on too long. By now Bella's texting someone something and they walk on in silence. Outside the Creative Writing Department they meet Mimi slouching on the stone steps in the sunshine, lighting a roll-up, smoke pulling out of her black lips. And here comes Wayne, miming smoking to make a point he's making about smoking. They are all assembled. Everyone's cardboard coffee-cup says the same word. They're just waiting for me.

*

A professor in Cambridge, I believe, baulked at the term 'creative' writing when he first heard it, and retorted that he would expect a 'creative' writer to come up with something like a new colour. You have to love that high threshold. As Bella, Ollie, Mimi and Wayne follow me up the winding stairs to Room 777 for their writing workshop, each looks quietly determined to make your regular blue, green, yellow and red seem stale compromises of the clueless past.

*

In the interests of Varsity balance, and also an apocryphal story I like to believe – a professor in Oxford, strolling across the Quad with another of his kind one day, was distinctly overheard to say the words: 'And, ninthly...'

*

So, ninthly, I ask for first lines from everyone. It's tried and tested, this exercise. It's very simple and always leads somewhere. In this case, as I'm making this up, I'll cut cards for which student came up with the best one. Wayne did. For Wayne, the whiteness is a playground and the blackness mischief. He calls himself a miscreant, he wants to miscreate, to *mischieve*. He composes on an iPhone and always goes with the auto-suggest. This is the line he's offered the class:

This is the end of the poem.

My exercise is that the other three now have to pretend they wrote that, and grow a second line organically from it. It has to sound like the same poet, the same world, the same view. Tonally, emotionally, formally, maybe non-formally, but it has to sound like the same poet. The idea is that you divest yourself of all your own prejudgments, preferences, inclinations. You pretend it was you.

So: is the poet indoors? Is this happening in the afternoon? Is there sun or rain? Is the poet looking at us? Those questions usually pay off – not so much with Wayne's line, perhaps, but it isn't meant to travel – anyway I'm just trying to get them going.

This is the end of the poem.

Ollie turns and says thanks a bunch mate that's impossible, Bella gazes at it doubtfully, Mimi makes that sighing noise that means Wayne is pissing away her time on earth. But they have to take it on. They have to take on its tone, its style, its pitch, and write a second line. Before Mimi can say *well my next line is blank* I say the next line isn't blank. Mimi. I leave them alone for a while and look out of a sunny window over the rooftops, then away at some buildings in the distance, thinking of long ago.

*

The poetic encounter is a meeting in life. Let it be like that, let it be that. Whether or not I achieve that myself, only time will tell and it won't tell me, but what I teach, all I teach, is how to aim there.

*

This is the end of the poem.

The whiteness in Room 777 bristles with thought. For Wayne the whiteness that follows the line he wrote himself is the speechless acclamation of all outsider artists. The world can see what he's done there. What now? But, as Dylan sang, 'to live outside the law you must be honest.' Wayne is honest, it all has significance, he will play the game. The whiteness becomes invitation, challenge, dare. His paper looks like this now:

This is the end of the poem.
This is the start of the poem.

In real life, when students have finished their assignments, I ask them to sit back with exaggerated smugness, so I know who's still working on it. They smile politely but I'm genuinely asking them to do that, it's helpful. Only I don't need to ask Wayne, he does it anyway.

Ollie notices Wayne has done that. He says 'It's alright for you, you wrote the first line.' Wayne murmurs at his coffee-cup: 'Not now I didn't, you did' and Ollie kind of thinks that's bollocks but grins, he got me, touché. *That's* why I came to uni.

For Ollie the whiteness is time without her. Bella, Isabella. It wasn't always and won't be always, but it is this morning. The whiteness is what hasn't been. The blackness what might be. The whiteness is she loves me. The blackness is not yet. The silence is Juliet's window up there, the noise is Romeo shinning up a drainpipe. And now Wayne's made that impossible with his post-this, post-that, pointless foolery.

This is the end of the poem.

Where could it possibly go from here? Where could *poetry* go? But as Ollie stares down the barrel of defeat at the hands of the postmodern, by and by he starts to be aware of darker tones he can use: now the whiteness is a cold world without poetry or love, any blackness he has left in him is suddenly heroic, the cry of a Grail knight through the fog. He dips nobly to the task, lances Wayne's full-stop so it bleeds into a comma, and the fight is on.

This is the end of the poem,
The loss of hope, the last failing of the crimson light in the
faraway west

(Ollie's not great on the line-break, we're working on it in our one-to-ones.) When he sits back, remembering to exaggerate the smugness because he loves to do the daft things I ask of the class, he really does feel pretty good. Wayne tried to close down the beauty in the world, but Orlando has foiled him from the heart of the tradition. 'Deeper magic from before the dawn of time', he remembers from *The Lion, the Witch and the Wardrobe,* and he jots that in the margin.

Isabella is sitting next to him and has forgotten he is in the world. I only mention that in case he was wondering. For Bella the whiteness is luminous, lunar, something she knows at night. The blackness is a secret, a secret from her. She has no feelings whatever about Wayne's line. Sitting here isn't being a poet, this is just a class *about* poetry. It's not pointless, this professor *knows* people. He knows poets who've been on TV. He has a Wikipedia page his daughter messes with. That's cute. In her notebooks in her room Isabella has nine hundred poems she hates, but last night she dreamed she was drunk among the True Poets, and all will be well.

> This is the – End of – the Poem –
> Death said – from his Carriage – Door

Bella's favourite poet is – oh come on. She remembers Ollie is in the world and she smiles at him when he smiles at her because she has good manners and she's written her line.

Mimi is drawing a really complicated maze no one can leave. She's pretending to be the girl in *Inception*. She finished this exercise in about eight seconds.

> this is the end of the poem
> said the idiot at the start

For her the whiteness was expectation and the blackness what you can fucking do with your expectation.

I say 'How are we doing, guys?'

*

Here's how I think they're doing. Wayne is right. He's always figuring out how far can things be taken. Always in the same direction, mind, but still.

Ollie's right. He feels deeply that a poem should have beauty, but so far he can only find that in the past. His whiteness needs to be stronger, blow harder in his face at the line-end, that will strengthen the black, curtail his time, make it worth more. He can dig for his beauties there. And anyway Bella smiled at him.

You think I know these people because I've taught them, but I know them because I've been them. One morning long ago in Boston town Professor Walcott said I played melodies with my right hand but my left hand just lay there. Another time, in his tiny wooden office on a Tuesday morning in November sunshine, he surveyed a forty-line lyric I'd written about me. He'd made us memorise Dylan Thomas's short poem 'Twenty-four years remind the tears of my eyes' and well, I'd had a birthday just that week, my 25th, so I'd done the obvious but gone on way longer. He frowned, ringed a little phrase with his pencil and then quoted with evident scorn: 'caving into sleep... caving into sleep? *caving – into – sleep?* Knowing what was coming, I said 'yes I suppose... that's pretty rubbish now I look...' He slid the poem back to me. 'It's terrific, the rest is shit.'

> Twenty-four years remind the tears of my eyes.
> (Bury the dead for fear that they walk to the grave in labour.)

In the groin of the natural doorway I crouched like a tailor
Sewing a shroud for a journey
By the light of the meat-eating sun.
Dressed to die, the sensual strut begun,
With my red veins full of money,
In the final direction of the elementary town
I advance for as long as forever is.

The students are looking at their professor looking out of the window.

*

Yes. Sorry. Bella is right too, she's right to love Emily Dickinson so much she can't help hanging round her room. Everyone should find one like that. When she gets clear of it she'll know a ton about form, whether or not she knows anything Emily knew.

And Mimi is probably a poet. She may not really be bothered, but having written

said the idiot at the start

and sat back, doodling in her book while recharging her Kindle, yawning and stretching in such a way as to make a cat seem diligent, she then suddenly shot forward like it mattered and changed it to

went the idiot at the start

because the line wasn't good enough, and she really couldn't bear it.

~

Form

Y OU MASTER FORM you master time. I repeat myself, writers write, pages turn, teachers teach. Regarding repetition, there is none in poetry, or at least what looks like repetition isn't repetition:

> The woods are lovely, dark, and deep,
> But I have promises to keep,
> And miles to go before I sleep,
> And miles to go before I sleep.

Recurrence of words isn't repetition. Ever. Try saying the above couplet in exactly the same way twice. Not only will you not sound like Robert Frost, you won't sound normal. The second line is likely to elongate, its last word probably fall in tone. Well let's exploit science to help us: the two sound-wave diagrams with their spikes and troughs are going to show skylines as different as Mecca's from Manhattan's. What's intervened between the two technically identical lines is *the need to say the same again*. Either side of that are different worlds. The relation of the two lines *to thought* is entirely different. One line outran thought, the second walks in step with it.

A line so grave, sublime and unbearable I can't even stand to contextualise it if you don't happen to know it –

> Never, never, never, never, never

– will show you there is no repetition in poetry.

*

You master form you don't master time, but what have you got that gets closer? Poems must be formed in the face of time, as we are. Whatever the whiteness is to you it's *also* time. As I said before, to me it's only time.

It can be time and God, as here in Gerard Manley Hopkins, where the poet's voice seems *held* in the arms of the Ineffable that bears it safely to and fro while allowing it to breathe, threading it with rhymes, chimes, alliterations – which sounds to me like a sense of God to a good Christian. By which I mean a good creature who's a Christian. The shrunken essence of the religious fundamentalist, with his beaming intolerance and immobile heart, is a *literary* one: he sees only the blackness of the Book, is blind to the whiteness. Hears what's in it for him and folks like him, is deaf to what surrounds it in time and space. That sounds to me like Pride in its pure form, dangerous, disgracing, and a sin among creatures.

Against which set this poet. See which words Hopkins puts at the edges; these words *know* they are edges, mortality is sounded:

> I am soft sift
> In an hourglass – at the wall
> Fast, but mined with a motion, a drift,
> And it crowds and it combs to the fall;
> I steady as a water in a well, to a poise, to a pane,
> But roped with, always, all the way down from the tall
> Fells of flanks of the voel, a vein
> Of the gospel proffer, a pressure, a principle, Christ's gift.

Time and the ocean, distantly breaking upon the ruminations of Matthew Arnold: 'Dover Beach', his most famous poem, was written in 1867, and it's one of the few poems of Arnold with any formal irregularities, as in these half- and quarter-lines; they simply cannot push further against the sound of the sea – the whiteness – so they break, fall back, and thought's sad glowing light comes in:

> The sea of faith
> Was once, too, at the full, and round earth's shore
> Lay like the folds of a bright girdle furl'd;
> But now I only hear
> Its melancholy, long, withdrawing roar,
> Retreating to the breath
> Of the night-wind down the vast edges drear
> And naked shingles of the world.

Or time and grief, as here in Thomas Hardy, with the lines curtailed, hemmed in by silence, the stanzas rubbing their hands together for warmth within but stubbed out by cold and sorrow:

> ...Leaves freeze to dun;
> But friends can not turn cold
> This season as of old
> For him with none.

> Tempests may scath;
> But love can not make smart
> Again this year his heart
> Who no heart hath.

> Black is night's cope;
> But death will not appal
> One who, past doubtings all,
>   Waits in unhope.

I use canonical examples because they have shown the strength to outlast time, a power I contemplate with awe. Most of the poets I draw from are called, inanely in my view, 'formalists': let's say they make new forms from old forms, what creature doesn't? We will know what 'free' verse means when we learn if it can survive. Let's recite some we know by heart, let's see how it's getting on. And by 'free' verse what I mean is verse that isn't formal at all, that neither shadows nor echoes it, has no interest in what it has foregone. Verse that on theoretical grounds has refused to engage with any traditional form at all. Which, in case you ask, means I don't mean Stein or Eliot or Pound or Jones or HD or Rosenberg or Williams or Bunting or Lowell or Plath or Morgan or Hughes. What I do mean is an awful lot of what we've got.

*

The Arnold, Hopkins and Hardy extracts display distinct attitudes to the left margin. The Arnold holds the familiar 'left-justified' line, the Hopkins sways symmetrically down the page (that stanza's from 'The Wreck of the *Deutschland*', which takes place mostly on a thundering sea), the Hardy uses indents to book-end his brief, numb stanzas. It's not hard to find reasons why those particular poets would shape those particular poems that way, but what I'd extrapolate is this: in most cases the left margin is playing the same part as, say, the fixed string in music, or the still canvas in painting, the concrete immovable against which the creaturely passion sings. Or, if you've a mathematical soul, shift a left-justified poem 90° and you have data bobbing from an x-axis. Indents or centre-justification really ought to have some rationale, and I'd extend that to those poems that roam freely about the whiteness.

The poet who takes that journey is assuming control of the whiteness, presuming a considerable amount of power, which also means advancing to the foreground of the poem's frame. We can see you, be aware of that. When this works – and some contemporary poets achieve it – it works because the poet is so extremely alert to what the blackness and the whiteness represent, what it means *apparently* to move freely. This level of skill is probably – I don't know everyone, this is my instinct – *probably* learned from reading and absorbing poetry considerably more formal. It was for Pound and Eliot. Maybe younger poets have figured out a shortcut.

No. If the poet thinks that unmooring from the margin or destabilising the space is a reward of freedom – and not precisely the opposite, a submission to mortality and the perilous closeness of chaos – the poem not only won't fly, it won't walk, it won't breathe. If you ditch the idea of any *fixity* – to say the least your heart beating or the top of the breath – without anything to show in its place, you have a sandcastle. It may be flying with twenty stiff flags of your intellect, but it's a sandcastle. The whiteness will come in like the evening tide upon your thought for the day, and we'll never know you had it.

*

But a coastal metaphor is too much in the sun. A sandcastle would have made a brief impression. A poem isolated from the functions of the body, throwing out allusions and in-jokes in code in a white space, is merely the brain at work, lodged in a dusty vault, parched and out of sight, nothing but data.

*

Indent is a form of punctuation, but a white one not a black one. Line- and stanza-break are the same: white punctuation. Any spaces you make on the page, you are dabbling in the element you don't know. So just – know that. Because all punctuation *is* is a polite request to time. And that's a huge thing to do, to address the deity.

So be aware. Here's a Punctuation Test.

One of the very few poems published by the reclusive Emily Dickinson is known – as her poems generally are – by its first line, 'A narrow Fellow in the Grass'. It's about a snake. It was published as 'The Snake' in *The Springfield Republican* in 1865. To Dickinson's dismay, the journal altered her punctuation.

You have to see the two side by side to fully comprehend the mess *The Republican* made of it. This is the first stanza:

Dickinson original	*Springfield Republican*
A narrow Fellow in the Grass	A narrow Fellow in the Grass
Occasionally rides –	Occasionally rides –
You may have met Him – did you not	You may have met Him – did you not
His notice sudden is –	His notice sudden is.

Only one thing is different. It looks tiny but as you see it's huge.

*

Take a poem you know well and tip the box of tricks over it: . , ; : ! ? ... – Let the little devils run riot. Run riot, run riot; run riot: run riot! run riot? run riot!!! Run riot??? run riot... *run riot...* run – Riot –

Blacknesses, forms, creatures...

*

I see these days, in young aspiring poets, a phenomenal complacency regarding form, a prejudice that allows them to arrive at adulthood having been convinced somehow that rhyme and meter and pattern are things of the past. I've met teenagers who with the solemnity of priesthood have jettisoned all the forms there are. Except for what – except for the form of a figure figuring there's no form.

That's all you have? What *you* reckon? What *you've* come up with? In the face of time?

*

I was judging a huge poetry competition once with thousands of entries, and a friend asked me how I could possibly get through them all. I said it took me only seconds to judge whether a poet was present. The friend was somewhat scandalised at what seemed a dereliction of duty, so I said – actually I didn't say, I just thought of saying later, in my car – I said he wouldn't ask that question of a concert violinist. A concert violinist could tell in seconds if a student knew his instrument from his elbow. When I think of the teaching of poetry, I invoke this Inner Violinist. If

I were a violin master at some fine arts academy, what would I think of a student who arrived at my class at 21 having decided there is nothing he or she can learn from long ago? No skills to develop. No moves to learn. No marvels to consider. Nothing to still you with its force. Okay let's hear you play. Or if a ballet dancer thought the same? Or a sculptor? Nothing to learn from work that outran time? Nothing of lasting value can come from one who thinks so. I don't think anything has, or will.

*

It's not hard to get how seductive it is finally to crash out through the gates of school into a place without constraints: the life-event is bound to be echoed in the mind. That *anything* goes now, if it's true to you it's true. But to feel that one is of the generation that has it right, that's making the sound that should now always be made, to behave as if the past has been corrected in your lifespan, whether that's in poetry or literature or art or public life – it offends time, the deity-I-go-by. You don't have to venerate time like I do, like a wryly cheerful monk, for that stance to look absurd.

Because some of you I'm trying to reach. Who've written a few poems but have no idea how they did or why, who've not yet considered those things. I'm trying to reach those whose poems I didn't judge in a few seconds – or I did, but I judged them worth the candle, like I heard you sing in the silence, or you could hold the bow to the string. I'm trying to reach you before your mind's made up, before you've decided – before you've done a damn thing – how the damn thing is done. Before you're a *something*-ist or swear by *something*-ism. Before you pin your colours to *anything-but-that*-ism. Before you've decided which long-gone poets were wrong all along, or which new kid on the block has been dead right for centuries. Before you start sounding how you think contemporary poetry should sound.

Now you may have a strong idea of what that sound is. We can all agree it's the sound of hundreds of birds singing. Anthologies of contemporary poetry are always called something that means the same as *Hundreds of Birds Singing*. But that sound, that general quirky chuckling back-slapping consensus, will be, to decades quite close by, something resembling quiet.

*

Read all the way back. Not everything. Let scholars do that. Travel back and make three stops. Hart Crane was formed out of Elizabethan playwrights, French Symbolists, and Walt Whitman. The sound is unique. From 'To Brooklyn Bridge':

> How many dawns, chill from his rippling rest
> The seagull's wings shall dip and pivot him,
> Shedding white rings of tumult, building high
> Over the chained bay waters Liberty –

> Then, with inviolate curve, forsake our eyes
> As apparitional as sails that cross
> Some page of figures to be filed away;
> – Till elevators drop us from our day.

Travel back and make three stops, but when you stop do stop. Read what made it. Read what's still here. No long-gone poets you can find in books or on websites are long-gone at all: if their pieces survived them they're poets. Work out why they are. Find out what time knows and you don't. No new kid on the block has yet *survived*: time knows more about that too, and it's in no hurry to tell.

The best we can do to learn is to learn from what lasted, like our kindred species learn: this survived because it was cunning, this survived because it was strong, this survived because it was lovely. The best we can do is read poems that outlived their makers, sad but so; we can hunt for clues to why. The second-best we can do is read up on the old stories – Greek, Hebrew, Roman, Norse, Celtic, Arabian, African, Amerindian – so we know a little of what these poets knew and their poems still know. And simply so we hear those stories, for real poets are campfire people.

*

Poetry forms in the face of time. The best place to see this happen is when time is at its hottest and most implacable: a time of terror.

> He's gone, and all our plans
>> Are useless indeed.
> We'll walk no more on Cotswold
>> Where the sheep feed
>> Quietly and take no heed.

Ivor Gurney was born in Gloucester in 1890, the second child of a tailor and a seamstress.

> His body that was so quick
>> Is not as you
> Knew it, on Severn river
>> Under the blue
>> Driving our small boat through.

He sang as a chorister in the cathedral there, and began composing music in 1911. His teacher Charles Villiers Stanford, who also taught Ralph Vaughan Williams, thought Gurney was hugely talented but 'unteachable'.

> You would not know him now...
> > But still he died
> Nobly, so cover him over
> > With violets of pride
> > Purple from Severn side.

Having enlisted as a private soldier in the Gloucestershire Regiment, he was working on his first book of poetry when he was wounded on the Western Front in April 1917. In September of that year he was gassed at St Quentin. This exacerbated an existing bipolar condition, and Gurney suffered several breakdowns after the war. The last fifteen years of his life he lived in mental hospitals.

> Cover him, cover him soon!
> > And with thick-set
> Masses of memoried flowers –
> > Hide that red wet

We are standing in a trench, in the line-break to end them all –

> Thing I must somehow forget.

*

Were poetry to be the only surviving record of a civilisation, the years of, and after, the First World War would tell us something terrible had come. This would be true whether or not we understood the language. Under Colchester, the oldest town in England, a stratum of charred black earth, what archaeologists call a 'destruction layer', is witness to the wrath of Boudicca. The forms of poetry fracture in the white heat of 1914-18. We see that change came suddenly everywhere.

We see it in the body of Gurney's poem, a pastoral lyric called 'To His Love', singed in a flash with nightmare – the modern world seems to dawn with a shudder in that line-break 'wet/Thing' – and we see it in this shocking revision Wilfred Owen – devotee of Keatsian beauty finding himself in hell – makes to some lines in 'Dulce et Decorum Est', turning from:

> If you could hear, at every jolt, the blood
> Come gargling black and frothy from the lung,
> And think how, once, his face was like a bud,
> Fresh as a country rose, and clean, and young...

To:

> If you could hear, at every jolt, the blood
> Come gargling from the froth-corrupted lungs,
> Obscene as cancer, bitter as the cud
> Of vile, incurable sores on innocent tongues...

The changes to the 3rd and 4th line are plain to see, but run the two alternative 'gargling' lines through your mind a while, and witness Owen's honesty, his witness, straining – *staggering*

– clear of decorum. Feel the poor tongue and teeth trying to process what he's seen.

But we see this terrible change, above all, in the forms. Of course the experimentation of Gertrude Stein and others predates the Western Front, and of course traditional forms don't vanish once the guns go quiet, but no other period of English poetry can show a tonal shift – lurch – quake – to rival *this*:

> Flame out, you glorious skies,
> Welcome our brave,
> Kiss their exultant eyes;
> Give what they gave.
>
> Flash, mailed seraphim,
> Your burning spears;
> New days to outflame their dim
> Heroic years...
>
> ...England – Time gave them thee;
> They give back this
> To win Eternity
> And claim God's kiss.

To *this*:

> Only a live thing leaps my hand,
> A queer sardonic rat,
> As I pull the parapet's poppy
> To stick behind my ear,

Droll rat, they would shoot you if they knew
Your cosmopolitan sympathies.
Now you have touched this English hand
You will do the same to a German
Soon, no doubt, if it be your pleasure
To cross the sleeping green between.

Both poets are Isaac Rosenberg, from 1914 and 1917, before the trenches and in them. Poetry forming, before our eyes and a rat's, in the face of time. Rosenberg perishes in 1917. Five years later

I think we are in rats' alley
Where the dead men lost their bones.

'What is that noise?'
The wind under the door.
'What is that noise now? What is the wind doing?'
Nothing again nothing.
'Do
'You know nothing? Do you see nothing? Do you remember
'Nothing?'

*

T.S. Eliot, for it is he, didn't think there was such a thing as free verse, because 'the so-called *verse libre* which is good is anything but free'. He goes on to assert that: 'the division between Conservative verse and *vers libre* does not exist, for there is only good verse, bad verse, and chaos.' I have resisted much quoting from poets on poetry, though the best of it (him, Coleridge, Frost, Auden, Jarrell, Brodsky) is magnificent, simply because I wished to grow this work outdoors, in plain view and morning light. Eliot, as a resource shallowly mined by prospectors seeking only certain nuggets, proves an exception.

He and Ezra Pound and the Modernists were in conscious revolt against what they saw as a stale late-Victorian formalism which dragged on into the Edwardian and Georgian years, and which seemed to them inadequate in the face of a world changed not only by the horrors of the Great War, but by industry, technology, mass culture, migration to the cities with its attendant miseries of poverty, anonymity, pollution. This is to simplify, but it's certainly a creed that several generations of young poets have carried with them, and continue to carry with them, into their literary milieux. And I don't have any argument with that creed at all, not historically and not aesthetically, and above all because it brought us the heights of Eliot and Pound and many who followed.

I just think a century's gone by and we're somewhere else in the story.

*

Is the young poet *still* to feel hurtled into a jagged new zone of speed and fuel and skyscrapers and faceless strangers? Is it still the future? Are we still so *alienated*? Six degrees of separation? We're one click from *everyone*. Beg, steal or borrow some cash and you could picnic on Uluru by the end of tomorrow. Rich folks have formed a queue for outer space. The Twin Towers go down and I get emailed poems about it *that afternoon*. There are nightclubs on aeroplanes and robots in the army. Yesterday's streamlined sci-fi creeps clanking into history. No one knows how anything actually works, or whose slaves are building it. I'm shy of fifty – just – and I've heard 'revolution' invoked on behalf of the MP3, the CD-ROM, the VHS, the cassette-player. My brothers and I, in our matching flares, huddled beside the PVC-clad oblong console our dad had brought home, all three astonished like Kubrick's apes around the black slab, as we fingered the bright green 'audio-cassette' that, if you pressed two heavy switches at the exact same time, could record me saying:

Glyn Maxwell! Bravo! Hip, hip, hooray!

or something, less than forty years back. That was the shock of the new, or it was that year. Only the elderly look stunned by change, and less so all the time. In fact they're starting to look mildly interested.

It seems to me, for all the global upheaval and environmental peril we face, all the violence and ignorance and waste and corporate banditry, that the bordered element we exist in, we literate folk of the Western world, this place we dwell in *day-to-day*, our music, our security, our likes, our flights, our cures, our designs, our wealth, our bloody comfort (I write this in a 'time of recession' but the phrase is just embarrassing in relative terms) – above all else the digital mesh we're snagged and tagged in for better or worse – that there is a roundedness to it all, an ease, a kind of antiseptic *sealed* quality to our time, as if we know new things will come, we read that amazing things will come, but the more that comes the less we actually *can* be amazed. *Pace* Victoria: we are *not* amazed. We just remember with nostalgia (see above) how once upon a time we were.

Well so much may be vague cultural supposition, but my strong suspicion remains that many young writers of the late 20th century, particularly in the West, developed styles and strategies of verse that were not an effect of social or political reality (like, say, the necessary coding of poets in the Soviet bloc or the four-square fury of the Black Arts Movement in the USA) so much as of literary history, or, to be less charitable, aesthetic inclination, that the once-vital, visceral responses of early Modernism have dwindled over a hundred years into thoroughly private habits.

*

Telling any kind of truth, making work that's tough, unforgettable, lovely – like every poem I've used so far – will demand new forms of verse from poets. Sonnets and strict iambic pentameters won't do the job they used to. The sound of verse evolves. Rhyme, which we'll come to, was newfangled in the Middle Ages. Many of the old forms – sestinas, villanelles – had a purpose centuries back but are no more than exercises now.

The sestina, in particular, those peculiar constructs of six six-line stanzas, each line ending with one of the same six words, and the poem ending in a three-line stanza (or tercet) using the same six words again, was invented in the late 12th century by the Provençal troubadour Arnaut Daniel. I don't know why or what for. For love, for fun, for show, for practice? I only mention it at all because it seems such a fixture of poetry-composition in schools – where such a thing still exists in a society costed for the City. Writing a sestina at school is the literary equivalent of time-honoured activities like pointlessly jumping over a box shaped like a loaf of bread, or saying 'Here' to prove you're there. Unable to imagine a situation that would ever suggest the sestina as a necessary means of expression, I swore never to touch the things, until one day, in a book called *The Sugar Mile*, I needed to write dramatic monologues for a garrulous barman, edging up and down his station conducting several conversations at once.

Barmen talk in sestinas, I discovered. I researched this extensively.

Certain forms abide, and it ought to fall to each new generation to remaster them, rework them for the times. Otherwise they enervate and wither, and you see poets turning back to a kind of defensive formalism born of nostalgia. It gets called the New one, like things that are like the Old one. It makes the case against it.

*

Still, better that than no form at all. How can formlessness help us? It is *alien*, we don't know it and it doesn't know us. Whatever formed us formed us out of it, *from* it. And it's hard to see how postmodernism will help, if it means verse that's only kidding. Or obscurity, if it's verse that's not even kidding.

Because Formlessness says time is broken, Postmodernism thinks it's come to a stop, and Obscurity can't even muster the nerve to look it in the eye. Three monkeys. Move on.

*

Out of the smoke, into the mist. Who knows what's up ahead? On a digital plane of infinite perfect copies, universal virtual access, monetary cost over human value, and no such thing as big society, in a marketplace where a binary psychology – winner/loser, hero/villain, delight/decrepitude, fame/oblivion

– seems to influence or infect all realms of life equally, I imagine, or vaguely hope, that some kind of strong patterned poetry might take hold, memorable, usable, mastered and free, emphasising the human individuated presence as against the virtual, the evasive, the scrambled, the conforming. The breath that moves the brain, not the brain that holds the breath. Someone fierce for the art, independent of the noise, implacable, some intelligent fury. Some punk enragé writing only of love. Some brilliant stand-up with more than half a soul. Something unfooled, disabused, noticing what's happening. It will speak to us clearly but not simply, with force and with depth. It will learn from screenplay, as great filmmakers learned from poets. It will storm back into theatre.

Or maybe it won't. To paraphrase what my teacher said when I interviewed him a few years back: if things go on progressing as they are in contemporary American poetry – which is what we were discussing – it will soon have, effectively, no readership at all.

*

I have no idea what will happen. Here's something Byron said to Isabella over tumblers of port in her dream, trying to assure her that no one would remember Wordsworth or Coleridge – 'all the Lakers' – in the future:

> Scott, Rogers, Campbell, Moore, and Crabbe will try
> 'Gainst you the question with posterity.

Actually she read that in his Dedication to *Don Juan*, but he said it again in the dream, still wrong about posterity, still having a good time.

Here's the great Mandelstam again, looking ahead more responsibly, looking at us, beyond us, from the 1930s, where he died:

> If we were to learn to hear Dante, we should hear the
> ripening of the clarinet and the trombone, we should hear
> the viola transformed into the violin and the lengthening
> of the valve of the French horn. And we should see forming
> around the lute and the theorbo the hazy nucleus of the
> homophonic three-part orchestra of the future.

New forms. But still, forms.

*

The class are back. I mean to spend hours moving short words millimetres backwards and forwards at the taxpayer's expense. I like to imagine all the taxpayers of the nation, me included, out there on the leafy avenue that leads to the Writing Program, lining up to give young dreamers the hard-earned money we'd planned to spend on crisps.

*

Spades: you're all alone. Hearts you're with a loved one but it isn't going well. Diamonds it's going well. Clubs you're in a crowd, you're with two others, two hundred, two million. Fetch a deck of cards, obviously.

Two, it's very hot. Three, it's very cold. Four you're near a fire of some kind. Five you're close to water. Six it's dawn, seven it's sunset, eight you're underground, in the Tube, in a dive, in a pothole, in your grave. Nine is rain, eugh, ten is snow, brrr. The Knave is going to be danger, the details are yours to know.

The Queen you're in a bed, doing something beds are good for. The King means you are sitting round a table, eating or talking or anything and the Ace? Death, if you draw it, or something supernatural. What do the Jokers mean, Wayne wonders and I say Wayne, take out the sodding Jokers.

I cut the cards while I'm writing this and here's what happened. Isabella gets the 2 of Clubs so she's somewhere hot with several people. Wayne gets the 8 of Clubs so he's underground with several people. Mimi draws the 3 of Hearts so she's in a cold place having a bad time with someone. Orlando gets the 7 of Spades so he's all alone at sunset. These ideal situations were drawn by chance.

What are we doing? First off it's a class. You have to generate text somehow, the taxpayers at the window are demanding it, so you might as well do it this way. 'That's so random', says Mimi, accurately for once. But I developed this simple system so that I'd never have to hear anyone complain of being blocked or having nothing to write about. These are fifty-two more or less everyday situations. They're easy to imagine.

And they can help outside of class, when one is actually trying to write something. W.H. Auden, when he was a schoolmaster, had a famous encounter with a pupil who said he wanted to be a poet. Auden asked why, and the boy said he had a lot to say. Auden wrinkled a brow that would one day be impossible to wrinkle further, and said he'd rather the boy said he just loved playing with words.

Personally, I had absolutely nothing to say till I was about thirty-four. I'd have been a disappointing messiah. But what I did for about twenty years from my mid-teens was play with words, so that by the time I had some things to say I had a pretty good idea how to. The violin, you see. You have to take the freaking thing out of its case.

Say Isabella wants to write a poem about feelings she had about that Jean-Luc at that campsite by the lake when she was fifteen in a thunderstorm. But she gets a few lines in and thinks she's not getting it right, it wasn't like that, he wasn't like that, it didn't feel like that. Say she gives up because she's failing by her own ideal. She'll never be a writer! She shuts her sliver of iSlab and heads out to the mall. That's the day lost when she could have been advancing as a craftswoman, as a maker, when she could have been playing with words.

Robert Frost used to quit after twenty minutes, if he felt he wasn't 'getting his way'. Play a game instead. Whatever, stay sitting. Cut a deck of cards. You can cut three cards for three stanzas. Cards come at you like stanzas, with corridors between them, or swirling air, raging water, hours, deaths, ages.

Now Isabella has a situation to begin with, no actual ideal to hold against it, no real-world cold-eyed *template* to give it stage-fright. She looks at the cards in her room on a sunny Saturday lunchtime and says aloud what they mean.

1. 'I'm happy with one other person, close to water.' (Five of Diamonds. Again, that's truly what came out when I cut, so she can go straight to her campsite memory. Weird, cards.)

2. 'I'm with several others in the rain.' (Nine of Clubs, remembering holiday France in school-day England maybe?)

3. 'I'm happy with one other person, but there is danger.'
   (Jack of Diamonds. Complicated reunion, bad news about
   to break?)

The situation grows in the space. It may well begin to
resemble something from her life – how could it not? – but it
won't be defeated by any competing account that the memory
has set in prose. She is essentially, and let these three words have
their solemn due for once, *making – things – up*. We don't know
what the situation was in Isabella's real life (Isabella isn't real but
you are) so all we have is the black on the white. It can grow
organically, it can grow from itself. It has no responsibility to
recollected events in life. Its only directive is to live as a poem.

Memory-catchers, not dream-catchers. Dreams are memory-
catchers, but so are these cards, with a whole lot more control.
You can divide all your childhood memories into those where
it's obvious why you've remembered – Barry hit you, Lucy
kissed you, a house was burning – and those where there seems
no clear reason why you've remembered – sunlight on a desk
with a leather-blue surface, a game of Lego soldiers in a bay
window, locking my bike to a rail by a greenhouse. A poem will
sometimes *suggest* why those memories stayed. At the very least
you'll be led somewhere. You'll be breathing around something
your body preserved. And, poets, your brain's in your body.

*

So playing cards conjure up something from nothing.
Equally useful, yet drawing strength from a deep existing well,
is translation. As pure exercise, translate not from a language
you know but from one you don't. An original in Xish, a blank
page or screen, and an English-Xish/Xish-English dictionary:

all you need. You find out what the Xish means, you make a rough prose version. Then, while noticing the form the Xish poet wrote in – quatrains, rhymes, nothing, whatever – but not necessarily copying it, you trust your instinct and choose the poem's *English* form. You versify your prose. A ghost takes shape in your room, it stills time as ghosts do, and, when it departs, with its soul and yours in eerie union, work has been done.

*

The students cut their cards, look a bit annoyed, sit back and wait for ideas. They have to write six lines, including at least one stanza-break. The third rule, which Wayne is proud to say I devised for his sake, is *don't do anything annoying.* Here's how they do:

> I was waiting for you by the old road
> with my arms round myself.
> Then I saw you you were running
>
> over the field to me
> but however fast you ran you were still
> small I was still waiting

*

> I stood – among so Many –
> who knew me there were – none
> who knew me – only One

whose Eyes – were like Money
he could – keep Forever –
All – he – could keep – Forever –

*

why are you here i

asked group-captain
jones as he was falling, ah

8 of clubs like u he went
same time tomorrow
morning eh

*

The crimson light is failing on the strand.
I reach out, but empty is my hand.
I used to walk on air, but now I walk on sand.

Where are you? I don't know. You are not here.
The light is fading. Day will disappear.
White waves are breaking by the ancient ruined pier.

*

Ollie folds up his lament-in-two-rhymed-tercets, breathes
deeply, moves the poem ruefully in the direction of Wayne like

he's passing a handcrafted Valentine to a shredder. But Wayne's to his right, and rules are rules. Wayne's goes to Bella, Bella's to Mimi, Mimi's to Ollie.

*

They have to make *a small change that makes a big change*. A word altered, a word moved, a margin moved, anything. The winner is the one whose slight change changes most.

Wayne says his first thought was to set Ollie's poem in London: 'The crimson light is failing on The Strand...' and make it a poem about an elderly disgraced aristocrat, 'the ancient ruined peer' but, having elicited a little groaning, and seen the patience of the poet in question gently ebb – 'strand is a word for beach actually Wayne' 'is it actually Orlando?' – Wayne says well then he'll let the tide rise and see what's left of the sandcastle:

Ollie	*Wayne*
The crimson light is failing on the strand.	crimson light failing
I reach out, but empty is my hand.	reach out empty
I used to walk on air, but now I walk on sand.	walk on , sand
Where are you? I don't know. You are not here.	you? I don't . You
The light is fading. Day will disappear.	fading disappea
White waves are breaking by the ancient ruined pier.	break ng y i

There's a silence as Wayne's tide comes further in. Ollie can't really see how he can apply that principle in general. Mimi likes what Wayne did; she says the rhymes loved themselves too much, it was all about the poet. Ollie says it *is* all about the poet.

Mimi says yeah that's why the girl dumped you and I move the discussion on.

Isabella says she isn't keen on 'fading disappear', it's tautological. Ollie, in love with her but at work here – and yes, he'll look up 'tortological' on dictionary.com as soon as class is over – protests to her he didn't write 'fading disappear'. Wayne says you did. Ollie says well, yes, but he wrote 'Day will' between them. Mimi says day's over though, *Orlando*, it's sunset now, though it's actually about time for elevenses, and the four of them sit back happily in their complementary styles.

*

Bella quite likes Wayne's effort, which makes Wayne look a little irritated, as he prefers people to look blank, it's how he knows he's functioning. But now she says straight out that he has the stanza-breaks all wrong. Meaning, murmurs Wayne.

Wayne	*Bella*
why are you here i	why are you here i asked group-captain
asked group-captain jones as he was falling, ah	jones as he was falling, ah 8 of clubs like you he went
8 of clubs like u he went same time tomorrow morning eh	same time tomorrow morning eh

The sunlight streams about tall Isabella... 'Meaning that the *i* knows it's going to ask group-captain jones the question, I mean, he's already asked it, *why are you here?* so there's no call for a stanza-break before *asked*, it's gratuitous, there's no call even for a line-break. The line-break before *jones* can work, because maybe the *i* needs an instant there to remember his name, which is actually quite funny, as all it is is, well, *jones* which everyone's called, and I'm also not sure about the stanza-break between *ah* and *8* because I think group-captain jones has this answer ready for anyone who asks him, because 8 is, sort of, his ID. And I'd break the stanza after *he went* so he can fall further through the sort of, nothingness they're falling through for some weird reason of Wayne's, and then, because he's got good manners, he says *same time tomorrow* etc.'

Wayne, honest Wayne, nods and says to her, only to her, and in earnest, which is valuable earnest as we don't meet it often: 'Interesting.'

'Because he wouldn't say *u*, he'd say it properly: *you*,' adds Isabella who's not done yet, and Orlando agrees. Wayne turns sharply to look at Orlando: 'Really? Why wouldn't he say *u*, Orlando.' 'Well,' says Ollie, and nothing comes. 'Because jones is a group-captain,' says Isabella, and her hopeless suitor beams and does the shrug that means 'Well, *duh*!'

'It's non-U to say *u*,' pipes up their professor, meaninglessly to them.

*

Nothing happens for a while, as Mimi pretends not to have realised it's her turn and is drawing a ringed planet. When she's ready she says to Bella without looking at her, for they get along okay but have nothing in common:

'Put them back, you should, put them back where you found them.'

'Excuse me?' Bella goes.

Wayne has a guess: 'Ms Dickinson's dashes.'

'She isn't watching you, Bell,' Mimi goes on in her vein, 'Emily isn't watching. Look. I've taken them all out for you, they're back in her sewing-box.'

And she passes this to Isabella.

Bella	*Mimi*
I stood – among so Many –	I stood
who knew me there were – none	among so many
who knew me – only One	who knew me, there were
	none
	who knew me.
whose Eyes – were like Money	Only one,
he could – keep Forever – all	whose eyes
he – could – keep Forever –	were like money
	he could
	keep forever. All
	he could keep forever.

'It's yours now, Bell,' says Mimi. Bella doesn't look like she thinks it's hers. She glances at me to see if this is being allowed. I decide to make this a Moment. I say Emily Dickinson's dashes are the silence in a house she never leaves. They're timbers. Bella looks blank. *Timbres*, I say, cleverly, stupidly. She looks sad.

I mean it's not your house, I say, and this soft-centred mysticism, along with the sunshine and she suddenly remembering her cool dream of Byron, seems to do the trick.

*

Ollie doesn't understand Mimi's poem. 'I like that about it, though.' Nothing happens, then suddenly, drawing strength from his sense of what Isabella would do, he digs deep:

Mimi	*Ollie*
I was waiting for you by the old road	Waiting for you by the old road
with my arms round myself.	with my arms round myself.
Then I saw you you were running	Then I saw you you were running
over the field to me	over the fields to me
but however fast you ran you were still	but however fast you ran you were st
small I was still waiting	small I was still waiting

'Well I've well, changed two things. I was thinking how she, Mimi, drew the 2, and the 2 is cold, and if it was cold, maybe she wouldn't say *I was*, she'd just start with *Waiting*, as that's all that matters right? The waiting. It's too cold to say *I was*. It's like – it's like you don't see someone's hands when they're cold and waiting somewhere.'

Mimi goes on drawing rings around her planet. Ollie goes on:

'So that was one change I did. And the only other one is: *field*. I changed it to *fields*, with an *s*, plural, because if you say *fields* – '

Mimi looks up at him sharply: 'It makes the person smaller.'

'It – makes him smaller, yes. Which – helps to make it colder.'

Mimi is still looking at him, like he just appeared at the table. I think she's about to say something friendly. She ought to.

'What makes you think it's a him,' she wonders, crossing out her planet.

*

Poetry workshops are fifty times less valuable to the poet whose work is being scrutinized than they are to those doing the scrutiny. The poet whose work is being discussed is a trembling tower of ego, taking the general personally or the personal generally, feebly inferring through a cloud of panic what he really thinks she really thinks and so on. But the poets discussing it are learning all the time. They have no dog in the fight. Folks do selfless things in the white spaces. They hunt there for the group.

*

Does he win? Mimi asks me and I say yes. He wins the prize of making coffee.

~

Pulse

I DON'T TEACH PROSODY. Iambs, dactyls, spondees, trochees. I was given a famous old course called 'Prosody' to teach at a famous old university in New York, but two weeks in I discovered I couldn't teach it, and four weeks in decided I shouldn't. So if you came to this book to find out what the funny Greek words mean, here's an observation and some suggestions. They're funny Greek words because they're *Greek* words, which ought to tell you that they were devised by people who spoke and wrote in a language other than English. See if you can guess which one. If you think every syllable in poetry is *only* stressed or unstressed, you must dwell in some binary realm where it takes 10 to tango, 11110 days hath September, and there must be 110010 ways to leave your lover.

If you need to know what an anapaest is in a hurry, use Google. If you want to know with dignity, obtain John Hollander's little book *Rhyme's Reason*. If you're up for working it out yourself, we go back to the house of Coleridge and these lines from 'Metrical Feet', which he wrote for his young son. The dashes are stresses, the squiggles are not, and the poet put them there:

```
-   ~   -   ~   -   ~   -
```
Trochee trips from long to short;

From long to long in solemn sort

```
-    -   -   -   -    -
```
Slow Spondee stalks; strong foot! yet ill able

```
- ~ ~   -   ~   ~   - ~ ~ - ~ ~
```
Ever to come up with Dactyl trisyllable.

```
~ -   ~   -   ~   -   ~ -
```
Iambics march from short to long –

```
~   ~  -   ~ ~   -   ~   ~   - ~ ~          -
```
With a leap and a bound the swift Anapaests throng;

One syllable long, with one short at each side,

```
~     -  ~ ~   -   ~   ~  -   ~  -
```
Amphibrachys hastes with a stately stride...

*

Teaching prosody to young writers is like putting a rock in their way. Now they think there's a high road and a low road. Learn the terms and you're saddled with them: you've a horse to control. Ignore them and you set a course to ignore any thing that requires *learning*: a thousand miles on foot, avoiding paths and signposts. When the high-road poet falls off his horse everyone laughs. When the low-road poet trips on a root no one notices. Neither event is good for the journey.

I want to suggest a middle way but my metaphor won't let me. There's still a rock in the way. Not a rock then, a river. Look what language did there. Swim across, get wet, keep walking.

*

There are reasons forms survive. In biology, history, chemistry and music, in physics, French, geography and maths. In double Games. Find a period in your timetable where that's not true. If you find one, skip that class. Haul your Kindle to the far edge of the school field. There are reasons forms survive.

So in poetry we look in wonder at the sonnet (poem of fourteen lines), the ballad (alternating lines of four and three stresses), or pentameter (line of five stresses), like a pianist hears Bach or a botanist gazes up at a redwood. Above all, in English poetry, we go back to meter itself, the rhythm of a line. I don't say you *can't* point out stresses and unstresses, I merely say there are infinite degrees of stresses and unstresses that the Greek nomenclature can't help with. I even disagree with a few of Coleridge's above, and the man's trying to help. But you can, *roughly*, point out stresses.

*

In terms of musical notation, one should think of the stresses – the beats, the meter – as the *bars*, not as the notes, not as the crotchets or minims or breves. The meter should be time passing in the background, not time marked in the foreground. As soon as the reader starts marking stresses on a line, intoning 'AY but to DIE and GO we KNOW not WHERE' you're not hearing what was composed.

For people who use 'formalist' as an insult think poets who use meter are counting crotchets when in fact we're passing through bars. People who think they *are* formalists probably *are* counting crotchets.

Ezra Pound, contemplating the stale iambics of late Victorian verse, urged that poetry be 'composed in the sequence of the musical phrase, not in the sequence of the metronome.' Well, musical phrases can show infinite variety and still be supported by a regular structure of bars, 4/4 can turn to 3/8 or 9/16 or 2/4 and turn back again. These are called *time-signatures* – what's poetic meter but time-signature? The metronome does its boring job, but only a fool – literally an idiot – would write upon its strokes. The sound *it* makes doesn't make it to performance. The bars are silent, the notes sound. It seems to me some poets extrapolate Pound's critique of late Victorian pentameters – or the general Modernist argument against metrical form – to include, frankly, Shakespeare.

Conventional prosody will tell you the beats fall like this, a trochee (DUM-da) then four iambs (da-DUM):

/   /   /   /   /

    Ay, but to die and go we know not where

This is Claudio in *Measure For Measure* suddenly faced with death. We can at least accord him the dignity of crying this line like a creature, not a teacher. So if you tap out the meter like a metronome while saying the line like an actual human, I think the beats fall something like this:

/   /   /   /   /

    Ay, but to die and go we know not where

If you then regularise your marks in space, the line elongates to something more like how it might be delivered:

/   /   /   /   /
Ay,   but to die...   and go   we-know-not where...

A thousand actors will have them a thousand ways. The point is that the beats are as likely to fall through silence as upon sound. Meter to the poets who know what they're doing is a silent skeletal frame on which a creature rides.

The fissure in writing poetry, the chasm between what I believe absolutely and doubt profoundly, is not between the 'metrical' (say Frost) and the 'musical' (say Pound) – which is a crude reduction of the work of both, albeit the kind of reduction writers in both camps have made ever since Robert and Ezra bickered on the pavements of Bloomsbury; the fissure is between having a governing aesthetic *like either* – or having no governing aesthetic at all, which leaves you with nothing but your next thought, or your latest feeling. That's an impulse which waited ninety years to find its true literary form. It's called a blog.

*

Poetry is creaturely. What survives in it echoes corporeal phenomena: the heartbeat and the pulse, the footstep and the breath. How it echoes is different in each language, in each culture, in each age: *Beowulf*, from around the year 1000, 'Old English', is unrhymed and alliterative, four beats to a line, a caesura (or gap) between them:

Hwæt! We Gardena   in geardagum,
þeodcyninga,   þrym gefrunon,
hu ða æþelingas   ellen fremedon.
Oft Scyld Scefing   sceaþena þreatum...

The Canterbury Tales, from the late 1300s, 'Middle English', is rhymed and metrical, five beats to a line:

Whan that aprill with his shoures soote
The droghte of march hath perced to the roote,
And bathed every veyne in swich licour
Of which vertu engendred is the flour;
Whan zephirus eek with his sweete breeth
Inspired hath in every holt and heeth
Tendre croppes, and the yonge sonne
Hath in the ram his halve cours yronne,
And smale foweles maken melodye,
That slepen al the nyght with open ye
(So priketh hem nature in hir corages);
Thanne longen folk to goon on pilgrimages...

Chaucer the well-travelled European helped to popularize that line in English; there's nothing inevitable about it, it's history, geography, migration, providence. The only reasonable generalisation is that certain forms survive extraordinarily intact, and the only worthwhile study the poet, as a *maker*, can make of poetry is – which forms survived and for what reason? Or, to turn that into practical gold as you dig it from the soil – which forms survive *and for what purpose*?

*

I wouldn't want to be thought an incorrigible generalizer. There actually *is* a surviving rhymed poem in Old English, it was found in the Exeter Book, that 10th century collection with all the riddles in it. This poem that rhymes is known to scholars of Old English as 'The Rhyming Poem'. Which kind of makes my point.

*

The lines below are the sixth and seventh stanzas of the most famous poem in English. It's certainly the most popular, though the following verses may be slightly less familiar:

> We have known you for years,
> Through the hopes and the fears,
> Through the good times and bad times,
> Through the laughter and tears.

> Through the sun and the rain,
> Through the joy and the pain,
> We have sung this song gladly,
> Now we sing it again.

The next verse is probably the most celebrated:

> Happy Birthday to you,
> Happy Birthday to you,
> Happy Birthday, dear [your name],
> Happy Birthday to you.

The twelfth verse is especially interesting because – look there's no twelfth verse and no sixth or seventh and no other verses at all, there's just 'Happy Birthday' and 'Happy Birthday' is like that because if it went on any longer than four lines it would get really annoying and by verse nine the child would have sunk her teeth in the cake.

The same applies to the *second* most recognizable song in English, which, as it happens, is 'For He's a Jolly Good Fellow'. Man you'd hate that guy by verse sixteen: 'For he's a fairly good golfer,/Yes he's a fairly good golfer' and so on.

In apology to anyone who was for the slightest instant taken in by my extra verses of 'Happy Birthday', I'm happy to point out that the second of the seven verses of a certain poem –

> Solemn the drums thrill; Death august and royal
> Sings sorrow up into immortal spheres,
> There is music in the midst of desolation
> And a glory that shines upon our tears.

Is probably less well known than the fourth –

> They shall not grow old, as we that are left grow old:
> Age shall not weary them, nor the years condemn.
> At the going down of the sun and in the morning
> We will remember them.

I think it's fair to say that time has eroded Laurence Binyon's 'For the Fallen' to the length it needed to be.

*

Because this is about *the time taken by forms*. Call it the 'Happy Birthday' principle. It applies to any poetry. Most obviously to a sonnet, as here in Shakespeare's 105th:

> Let not my love be called idolatry,
> Nor my beloved as an idol show,
> Since all alike my songs and praises be
> To one, of one, still such, and ever so.
> Kind is my love today, tomorrow kind,
> Still constant in a wondrous excellence;
> Therefore my verse, to constancy confined,
> One thing expressing, leaves out difference.
> 'Fair, kind, and true,' is all my argument,
> 'Fair, kind, and true,' varying to other words;
> And in this change is my invention spent,
> Three themes in one, which wondrous scope affords.
> 'Fair, kind, and true' have often lived alone,
> Which three till now never kept seat in one.
> For, were my love a love of lesser kind,
> Fair by occasion, true by choice or need,

No. Stop. That's me pretending, those are my lines. You knew that. Shakespeare knocked off after 'seat in one'. It's a sonnet. It doesn't have to stop *because* it's a sonnet. It's a sonnet *because it has to stop.*

The sonnet (Italian, 'little sound') originates as a poem of love – even when John Donne or George Herbert or Gerard Manley Hopkins requisition it for the Lord it serves as a poem of love – and a poem of love must share the world with that which its maker loves. Its whiteness is vivid, dazzling, its black creature there for a brief interlude of grace. For what its maker loves is, in the case of love, its lover, and, in the case of God, its Maker. Both lover and Maker demand time of the poet: for sex or prayer, if nothing else. Put bluntly: given that you feel or think *that* – do you not have somewhere else to be? Something else to be doing?

So built into the sonnet is its sense of an ending, a decorous, measured conclusion that leads back to the lover: 'And yet to times in hope my verse shall stand,/Praising thy worth, despite his cruel hand.' Or back to the Maker: 'Except you enthral me, never shall be free,/Nor ever chaste, except you ravish me.' Now the tones of *those* addresses are curiously similar...

Of course, many sonnets, not least Shakespeare's and Donne's, who between them wrote the greatest, are poems of anguish, love betrayed or ended, and many deal with religious doubt or political fear: yet they hold their shape, evoking and echoing the light they cannot face or the ideal they mourn the loss of. They are turned from, back to the matter of life.

*

Let's elaborate on a comparison made earlier. The sound of Shakespeare addressing a lover serenely, as a constant, in the famous 18th Sonnet:

> Shall I compare thee to a summer's day?
> Thou art more lovely and more temperate:
> Rough winds do shake the darling buds of May,
> And summer's lease hath all too short a date...

These are pentameters. Salt them with your prosodic stress-marks and unstress-marks if you like – try doing that with 'This music crept by me upon the waters' from *The Tempest* if you really want to put a fence round fireflies – I'll settle for saying there are roughly five beats to each line.

In Marvell's 'To His Coy Mistress', a poem where the love and lust are explicitly unrequited, at least for now, there are clearly four beats to a line. These are rhymed tetrameters, a galloping measure:

> Now let us sport us while we may,
> And now, like amorous birds of prey,
> Rather at once our time devour
> Than languish in his slow-chapped power...

What might we *infer* from the distinct meters and the distinct rhymes? *Infer* isn't quite right, a shade too cerebral: we receive these lines on a deeper level. It's plainer to wonder what we *feel*. To take a phrase from Wordsworth, what's 'felt along the heart'?

Earlier, I said it helps to mist one's eyes when first contemplating a poem, see what's being told by shape alone. One can play the game with sound, turn the syllables to *dum da dum* in your ear a while, so the *formal* distinctions strike more clearly. Robert Frost suggested that one could hear a conversation in the next room, muffled through a wall, make out not a single clear word, and yet still understand what's going on. He calls it the 'sound of sense' and it's as much sense as I've ever read anywhere.

The pentametrical sonnet; the tetrametrical lyric... Five-stress Shakespeare, four-stress Marvell... In general I think the shorter the meter the more it's making of its poetic nature, its *performed* quality. At heart the Marvell and the Shakespeare are worlds apart rhythmically because Shakespeare *has* his love, and Marvell's still in the hunt. Marvell's meter is dancing for his desires, Shakespeare's is seated, in the company of something that would love it even silent.

Stretch the point to prove its strength: in this e.e.cummings poem from the 1930s we listen in on a situation akin to that of Marvell and his Coy Mistress, but the strict rhyming dimeters (two-beat lines) take us straight into light comedy: 'may i feel said he/(i'll squeal said she/just once said he)/it's fun said she...'

Short rhyming meters tend to bring the poem-as-poem and the poet-as-poet to the foreground. The more obvious the shape, the clearer the maker's mark on it. At the most playful extreme you can file limericks here, clerihews and so on. Contrariwise, rhymes turn comic by *lengthening*, as the work of W.S. Gilbert attests – though in poetry no one's ever really topped Byron's little turn from *Don Juan*: 'But O, ye lords of ladies intellectual,/ Inform us truly, have they not henpeck'd you all?'

*

What matters most in rhyme is how soon the next one comes. (Of course in the cummings this is played for joke-effect.) In the Marvell they come thick and fast, with urgency, to seize and hold attention. There's a directness: *this/which goes with this!/ that/which goes with that!* Sexual, of course. A naked shape.

The addressee in Shakespeare's sonnet isn't going anywhere, is persuaded already, so the quality of attention is different. The rhymes in sonnets – either of the two main forms of sonnet – see Google, see Hollander – return in time, sometimes in the next line, maybe two or three lines later. *This/and that.../reminding me of this/reminding me of that...* Lovers' talk. The complexity, the 'woven' quality, creates a sense of something made before, patterned in advance for pleasure. A clothed shape.

*

Another example. The ballad-form, combining short stanzas and strong rhymes, is built to tell memorable stories. Metrically ballads are always emphatic but line-length and rhyme-scheme are flexible. Wordsworth's 'Lucy Gray' alternates four-beat and three-beat lines, the classic form:

> Oft had I heard of Lucy Gray:
> And, when I crossed the wild,
> I chanced to see at break of day
> The solitary child.
>
> No mate, no comrade Lucy knew;
> She dwelt on a wide moor,
> – The sweetest thing that ever grew
> Beside a human door!

Simple tale at first look, quickly recurring rhymes, and a cliff-hanging quality to the stanza-breaks, as if the listening audience needs the space to absorb what's happened and be ready for what's next. There's 'The Rime of the Ancient Mariner' of course, but we're on a break from him. Here in 'La Belle Dame Sans Merci' Keats varies the form, most notably truncating the fourth line, to suggest something lost, undone, gone wrong in the world:

> O, what can ail thee, knight-at-arms,
>   Alone and palely loitering?
> The sedge has withered from the lake,
>   And no birds sing.

Which ominous information settles into the whiteness. The antiquity itself plays a role. Those strong meters and rhymes, those vivid stops for breath – which is likely to be the very origin of stanza-break – all suggest an ancient story too powerful to go untold, a tale that has risen out of the past, and which the teller can only helplessly transmit. Folk music, of course, hands stories down the centuries this way. The Anglo-Scottish ballad 'Lord Randal' – 'O where have you been, Lord Randal, my son?/O where have you been, my bonny young man?' – versions of which also exist in Danish, German and Hungarian – turns in the hands of Bob Dylan to 'A Hard Rain's A-Gonna Fall', deriving huge force from that *received* quality, as if unarguable truth is being told by a traveller come to us from faraway through a mist.

Emily Dickinson writes virtually everything in ballad form, although uniquely she delays and divides and opens out her thoughts with those dashes, gives them height and weight with capitals, and frequently modifies her rhymes to half-rhymes, as if the idea were caught in passing, and were changing as it left her. I think the ancient force of the ballad-form impersonalises, deepens her poems, makes for a sense of universal wisdom caught briefly on the wing:

> The difference between Despair
> And Fear – is like the One
> Between the instant of a Wreck –
> And when the Wreck has been –
>
> The Mind is smooth – no Motion –
> Contented as the Eye

Upon the Forehead of a Bust –
That knows – it cannot see –

Many poets – Donne, Herbert, Hardy, Auden, Moore, Plath – are so formally adventurous or restless that they invent new stanza-forms, new combinations of line-length and rhyme-scheme, with almost every poem, as if willing the poem, *daring* the poem – to grow itself around the matter.

*

Let's see what we find scrunched up on the factory floor.

My poem
    doesn't know where to go so it goes here
and finds its subject suddenly quite clear
but what to say
next? I have no idea,
    so I'll end the stanza in this thoughtful way

then start
    this new one oh! with a memory I've had
that really nails it, really makes me sad
but also, now I think,
wasn't all that bad,
    and something something ink? ice-rink? zinc? drink?

In the years I didn't know anything I used to roll dice to choose the forms of line and stanza. 4 beats, 4 beats, 5 beats, 2 beats, throw a 6 for a stanza-break; toss a coin to rhyme or not. See what kind of thoughts come, what sounds come. What about long lines suddenly cut short? What about indents? What

if it's rhymed here and there, or what about there and here?
What alters then, what shifts? Tonally, emotionally? What if it's
not rhymed at all?

> I look at something,
> but obviously it reminds me of something else.

> Which I saw once,
> somewhere way more interesting than my room is.

> So I carry on like this,
> until I guess I've created a sort of mood.

> Then I'm just about ready to end
> on some striking point that makes you think a bit.

Factory floor, shop-window. Know the difference. Take the
pressure from yourself. Apprenticeship, not sales team. No one's
looking. Work, explore. What form suggests what story? What
kinds of light are shed by rhyme and rhythm?

> I'm confident the poem I start
> will tell you all about my heart,
> it's rhymed so you can have no doubt
> the truth will come completely out
>   at last, but then again

> she doesn't care, and what is worse
> already it's the second verse,
> I'm saddled with this thumping scheme

I can't keep up. I feel a dream-
    sequence coming on...

Pick up your violin is all I'm saying.

*

In every case above (before I began my dumb limbering-up), poets living *now* – for *now* is when it was for them – found ways to make old forms – lines, meters, rhyme-schemes – come alive again in the present. Who now, in *your* now, makes the strong rhyme breathe again? The rap artist, for one. Rap rhymes for show, for fun, for power. Why is rap the shape it is? Why doesn't it pause for breath? Because it's an urban form, it formed with others standing close, itching to interrupt it, to break it, best it, it won't stop till it's had its say: *This-and-hey-this-and-how-about-this-and-then-this-and-also-this-and-hell-yes-this!* It wants you to feel it was conjured into life, whipped up under pressure, not handed down, owing nothing, made up *right now.* New forms yes. But forms, and reasons for them.

*

You can't really have a clue what English poetry's been through without getting a brief reductive history of the pentameter – the line that takes the time of a breath – so here comes mine. Followed by where it took me next.

The classical Latin line of twelve syllables flows into Old French *chansons* (*The Song of Roland* and so on), through the 12th-century troubadours of Provence beloved of Ezra Pound, to the Italians Dante, Boccaccio, Petrarch. In each case the native language adapts in terms of syllable-count and caesurae (pauses mid-line) – for example in Italian it almost always has eleven syllables, because most Italian words have 'feminine' endings (they end on an unstressed syllable: *bene, dolce, arrivederci*). In the hands of Chaucer, English man of letters home from the Continent, it's five beats or stresses, the *iambic* rhythm (all right, all right – da-DUM da-DUM da-DUM da-DUM da-DUM is a *pure* iambic pentameter) which comes to the fore.

Chaucer's fame, and the status of *The Canterbury Tales* as the first great poem in English, establishes this five-beat line at the heart of English poetry. It passes to the 16th-century sonneteers Wyatt and Surrey, thence to Philip Sidney and Edmund Spenser and on to the great Elizabethan and Jacobean playwrights, not least Christopher Marlowe who, as Ben Jonson wrote, forged the 'mighty line' for the English stage; after which comes Jonson himself, Webster, Fletcher, Shakespeare. He, like any poet finding freedom in form, constantly varies the placing of the stresses, and at one point writes a line with no iambs at all. We had it before – King Lear, clasping the body of his hanged daughter –

Never, never, never, never, never.

The pentameter dominates thereafter, in the hands of 17th-century Milton generally unrhymed (or 'blank'), 18th-century Pope and Dryden generally rhymed in couplets, and the 19th-century Romantics, who mostly rhymed it – with the exception of Wordsworth's autobiographical *The Prelude*, written in meditative blank verse. The Victorians see no reason to change anything much, Browning, Tennyson, Swinburne (Hopkins stands alone, we'll come to him; Meredith's a treasure you can find for yourself) at which point the pentameter arrives in the Modern City.

On go the Edwardians and Georgians and the 'War Poets' destroyed or transformed or both in the trenches, but by the early 1920s the great pentametrical river is a backwater, a canal by a warehouse. The wave of Modernism breaks: the experiments of Gertrude Stein, the Imagists (Ezra Pound, Hilda Doolittle), the Symbolists, and the psychological wreckage and despair left by the fighting – together change the cultural landscape forever, and – we're looking from a distance here, so we only make out peaks, or rather, tall buildings – poetry in English is altered for keeps by T. S. Eliot's 'The Love Song of J.Alfred Prufrock' and 'The Waste Land'.

Ezra Pound famously wrote: 'Breaking the pentameter, that was the first heave' and the world (or rather the campus) is still filling up with young poets who inexplicably believe a poem like 'Prufrock' – 'We have lingered in the chambers of the sea/By sea-girls wreathed with seaweed red and brown,/ Till human voices wake us, and we drown' – was somehow breaking the pentameter. 'The Waste Land' is strewn with bits of lines, fractured forms: the majority of it is written in some kind of meter. There are pentameters, couplets, dimeters, songs, dialogue, blank verse. It's really a crate of fragments, a fearful and beautiful mosaic of all that's gone before – like 'The Oxen of the Sun' chapter in Joyce's *Ulysses*, which is told in a compendium of English prose styles from Anglo-Saxon alliterative to future slang. Anyway no poem teaches better than 'The Waste Land' how a poet should confront the past (as indeed no essay teaches better than the same poet's 'Tradition and the Individual Talent') but this lesson is misprised in every generation. You don't try to write in the style or perspective of men and women of the 1920s. You learn what went before you, you see what it all came to. Then you raise your voice.

And of course, if we stick to pentameter, there's W. B. Yeats in Ireland and Robert Frost in America, broad rivers running with the old forms, mastering and remaking. Even in England there's Auden still to come, and Larkin. It runs through the late 20th century in Ireland with Heaney, Longley, Mahon, farther afield in Walcott and Murray – the widening stretching *sunlit* pentameters – and on into my generation on these British isles right now. Where the work of a few British poets – they know who they are – shows a sustained, rewarded faith in the line of five beats, the line that takes the time of a breath. My work does for sure. But I dwell on Eliot and High Modernism and this early 20th-century fracture because of its huge and disproportionate effect on the century that came, on young poets ever since.

There's a different stream you can follow.

*

Old Man, or Lad's-love, – in the name there's nothing
To one that knows not Lad's-love, or Old Man,
The hoar-green feathery herb, almost a tree,
Growing with rosemary and lavender.
Even to one that knows it well, the names
Half decorate, half perplex, the thing it is:
At least, what that is clings not to the names
In spite of time. And yet I like the names.

These are the first eight lines of Edward Thomas's 'Old Man', written in 1914, before he volunteered for the Western Front.

What happens in these eight lines? A man remembers two names for a plant, but is struck by how leached and *unright* the words are. That's pretty much all that happens. Once you've checked the botanical facts (pointless, Thomas knew the countryside like no writer before or since) you'll see there's nothing else alluded to. It's just a man and his thoughts. In the first two lines the two names – absurdly contrary descriptions for one plant, 'Old Man' and 'Lad's-love' – are repeated, as if that could give them edges. He describes what it looks like, where it grows; he comes back to the names because the thought has persisted. In the 6th line he gets bogged down in Latinate words about it, or in fact words *about* words about it – 'decorate', 'perplex' – but is left clasping an empty Anglo-Saxon vessel: 'the thing it is'. What follows, let's not forget, is a *pentameter*:

At least, what that is clings not to the names...

How does one say that line? 'At least – what *that* – *is* – clings – not to the *names*? Perhaps. The lips, the tongue, the throat, the *brows*, all are working, willing to know, falling short of it.

Technically, it's a pentameter like these are: 'I'll leap up to my God – who pulls me down?' 'And flights of angels sing thee to thy rest...' 'To justify the ways of God to man...' 'Season of mists and mellow fruitfulness...' 'If I should die, think only this of me...' 'And each slow dusk a drawing-down of blinds...' Those are lines I used to look at like I look at stained-glass windows. But when I heard this – 'At least, what that is clings not to the names' – what I heard was the mind, *my* mind at work, I heard English now. This mighty line, this magnificent engine of English poetry, this monument, this pentameter, wasn't gold, or satin, or stained glass, or marble: here and now it was light. Light meeting the mind, recorded on the breath and returned in thought – or half-thought – *or no thought at all.*

> The herb itself I like not, but for certain
> I love it, as some day the child will love it
> Who plucks a feather from the door-side bush
> Whenever she goes in or out of the house.
> Often she waits there, snipping the tips and shrivelling
> The shreds at last on to the path, perhaps
> Thinking, perhaps of nothing, till she sniffs
> Her fingers and runs off. The bush is still
> But half as tall as she, though it is as old;
> So well she clips it. Not a word she says;
> And I can only wonder how much hereafter
> She will remember, with that bitter scent,
> Of garden rows, and ancient damson-trees
> Topping a hedge, a bent path to a door,
> A low thick bush beside the door, and me
> Forbidding her to pick.

Nowhere else do I find such a combination of plain language and complex perception. Nowhere do I find time and memory so active. Or the aged pentameter refreshed so skilfully, so subtly. In the sixth line of that extract, why does he say 'at last' and not just 'shrivelling/The shreds on to the path'? Because the extra syllables allow the shreds longer in the air. It's the time they take to reach the ground. This is what form allows, for the fixed string sounds the note.

Is there anywhere a more delicate and devastating characterisation of a child growing away forever from a parent than this, line-breaks and all: 'perhaps/ Thinking, perhaps of nothing...'? And now, with what barely breathed and creeping terror does he place himself there, where she was just now, where he was long ago, where they both were long ago. Nowhere in all of poetry do I find an agonising abyssal emptiness such as Thomas has in the two words 'Once more' – he tries to make the rest of that line last forever.

> As for myself,
> Where first I met the bitter scent is lost.
> I, too, often shrivel the grey shreds,
> Sniff them and think and sniff again and try
> Once more to think what it is I am remembering,
> Always in vain. I cannot like the scent,
> Yet I would rather give up others more sweet,
> With no meaning, than this bitter one.

Thomas's best friend was Robert Frost, who called him 'the only brother I ever had,' whose work his resembles, and with whom he walked many miles of Gloucestershire in the summer of 1914. Thomas had never written a poem when they met. It was Frost who, on reading prose like this, suggested Thomas work it up into verse.

> As for myself I cannot remember when I first smelt that
> green bitterness. I, too, often gather a sprig from the bush

and sniff it and roll it between my fingers and sniff again
and think, trying to ~~remember~~ discover what it is that I am
remembering. [~~but in vain.~~] I do not wholly like the smell,
yet would rather lose many meaningless sweeter ones than
this bitter [~~unintelligible~~] one of which I have mislaid the
key.

Robert also made the suggestion that, instead of enlisting,
Edward emigrate to Massachusetts with his family, but that one
wasn't to be.

See with what lightness and care Thomas has lifted prose into
verse. He has taken the thought and feeling of the black creature
and let the whiteness surge and flow around it, turned thought
and feeling back into pulse and breath, so that we hear nothing
but human sound, half of which is silence. The sound of you
breathing. He was killed in March 1917, by the blast of a shell,
near Arras. Ted Hughes called him 'the father of us all.'

> I have mislaid the key. I sniff the spray
> And think of nothing; I see and I hear nothing;
> Yet seem, too, to be listening, lying in wait
> For what I should, yet never can, remember:
> No garden appears, no path, no hoar-green bush
> Of Lad's-love, or Old Man, no child beside,
> Neither father nor mother, nor any playmate;
> Only an avenue, dark, nameless, without end.

~

Chime

It doesn't matter what this next passage means. Look for the alliterations, and look for the rhymes. You can easily spot rhymes in, say, Russian Cyrillics, just by squinting at the shapes of the words. What the following teaches us relates to the evolution of English hearing.

> SIÞEN þe sege and þe assaut watz sesed at Troye,
> Þe bor□ brittened and brent to bronde□ and askez,
> Þe tulk þat þe trammes of tresoun þer wro□t
> Watz tried for his tricherie, þe trewest on erthe:
> Hit watz Ennias þe athel, and his highe kynde,
> Þat siþen depreced prouinces, and patrounes bicome
> Welne□e of al þe wele in þe west iles.
> Fro riche Romulus to Rome ricchis hym swyþe,
> With gret bobbaunce þat bur□e he biges vpon fyrst,
> And neuenes hit his aune nome, as hit now hat;
> Tirius to Tuskan and teldes bigynnes,
> Langaberde in Lumbardie lyftes vp homes,
> And fer ouer þe French flod Felix Brutus
> On mony bonkkes ful brode Bretayn he settez
> > wyth wynne,
> > Where werre and wrake and wonder
> > Bi syþez hatz wont þerinne,
> > And oft boþe blysse and blunder
> > Ful skete hatz skyfted synne.

By now you can see it alliterates strongly in the long lines without rhyming. It rhymes only in the five short lines that follow: *wynne/wonder/perinne/blunder/synne.*

This is the opening stanza of the anonymous late 14th-century *Sir Gawain and the Green Knight,* written in a North-West-Midlands dialect of Middle English. Of its many splendours, one is at the heart of the matter: how the poem sits on a high hill between the rural alliterative past of English poetry – *Beowulf,* 'The Seafarer', 'The Battle of Maldon' – and its metropolitan rhyming future.

Two hundred years down the road, by way of Chaucer, Sidney, Spenser and the like, rhyme and pentameter rule, while alliteration is summoned in motley, as helpfully presented for your delectation here by certain amateur actors:

> Anon comes Pyramus, sweet youth and tall,
> And finds his trusty Thisbe's mantle slain;
> Whereat with blade – with bloody, blameful blade –
> He bravely broached his boiling bloody breast...

Peter Quince in full cry. Theseus, Hippolyta, Lysander and the rest, urbane Europeans who like to rhyme when they leave a room, smile with indulgence.

*

Your kinsfolk once trusted alliteration to pass on news, story, warning. Your kinsfolk reckoned rhyme absurd, discordant, an intruder. Your kinsfolk held rhyme to be the only source of beauty, alliteration a silly throwback. And now your kinsfolk think rhyme is sepia, Modernism stark black-and-white, and whatever he or she did this morning high-definition colour.

*

At any point in the evolution of any language, certain words connect aurally in a way that has nothing to do with meaning. You may turn your back on this wealth if you choose, but it won't stop shining. And because this is language and not capital, you could have taken all you could carry. Not a jewel of it would be gone. The poor passer-by might ask in puzzlement why don't you make yourself rich, and you say – what *do* you say? That you don't want it because you didn't make it yourself? Can life be nothing but self-made?

You'd stand out there below the stars, shaking your head as it says it doesn't see a scorpion, a huntsman, a fish. But they're there. They're there.

*

The *Gawain*-poet holds great treasures in balance. All the poem's stanzas are shaped like the one above, but the number of unrhymed alliterative lines is ever in flux, from about twelve to about twenty-four, while the five short lines that conclude every stanza – formally knows as the 'bob' ('wyth wynne') and 'wheel' (the other four lines) – remain constant throughout. The alliterative lines tend to push the story on; the rhymed 'bob and wheel' often draw back, in space or time, recap, sum up. Sometimes it sounds like an old villager is telling the story, then his son who's been to the town adds a little context, leans into the foreground, knits the thing together. Here are those things at work in Simon Armitage's vital retelling:

> With a tug of the reins he twisted around
> and, head still in hand, galloped out of the hall,

so the hooves brought fire from the flame in the flint.
Which kingdom he came from they hadn't a clue,
no more than they knew where he made for next.
             And then?
        Well, with the green man gone
        they laughed and grinned again.
        And yet such goings on
        were magic to those men.

Alliteration brings this; rhyme brings that. As a craftsman
the poet is asking himself what all true poets ask themselves:
*what forms survive for what reason? What forms survive for what
purpose?*

Just as our language shows the various arrivals or survivals of
Celts, Angles, Saxons, Vikings, Normans and everyone since,
our poetry develops alliteration, moves past it into rhyme,
moves past that into something, anything? Who knows. History,
geography, migration, providence. There is no more natural
reason for poetry to be alliterative than there is for it to rhyme.
In one age English words are drawn together by beginning with
the same sound; in another they are drawn together by sharing
the same vowel and final consonant. There is an arbitrariness, a
chance to it all. The constant is that words are *drawn together*. In
other languages other words. In other cultures other ways.

On the isles of Britain now, in the early 21st century, there are
perfectly good reasons not to rhyme. There are reasons to rhyme
sometimes, to half-rhyme and to not rhyme. But to oppose
rhyme as arbitrary, as some kind of compromise your mind
makes with language, is not only to traduce your language in its

present form, unimaginably deeper, stronger and brighter than you are, it's to go up against history, ancient history, pre-history.

Words were drawn together at a time of which you know nothing. You didn't draw them together and you can't pull them apart.

To rhyme – or indeed to alliterate, because I argue for form itself, not certain types of it – is to embrace the unknowable antiquity of your language, to breathe an entire element in the form of its local mist. So history, geography, migration and providence drew these words together in my hearing – *so be it.*

*

Next, here, amazingly, is a sonnet from 1877 that concentrates the entire history of English verse, alliterative and rhyming, as if both remain vibrant and constant, and to hand. Perhaps it takes somebody who believes profoundly in an element vaster than self – a believer, in fact, like Gerard Manley Hopkins – to gaze past fashion and tradition into the timeless heart of the language:

> As kingfishers catch fire, dragonflies draw flame;
>> As tumbled over rim in roundy wells
>> Stones ring; like each tucked string tells, each hung bell's
> Bow swung finds tongue to fling out broad its name;
> Each mortal thing does one thing and the same:
>> Deals out that being indoors each one dwells;
>> Selves – goes itself; *myself* it speaks and spells,
> Crying *What I do is me: for that I came.*

I say more: the just man justices;
　　Keeps grace: that keeps all his goings graces;
Acts in God's eye what in God's eye he is –
　　Christ. For Christ plays in ten thousand places,
Lovely in limbs, and lovely in eyes not his
　　To the Father through the features of men's faces.

*

If you are an aspiring poet under thirty, and you'd like to get a sense of how it would feel at a young age to believe profoundly in an element vaster than yourself, you could do worse than the modern equivalent of what Hopkins did and move every poem you've written so far to the Recycle Bin. Then empty it.

*

Let me put this question to a sceptic, to one who thinks, or has been taught by one who thinks, that rhyme is archaic, obsolete, unnecessary or – to park in the cornfield of the feeble-minded-right-wing: have you come to this conclusion after having worked with it? Not for years, not for months, not even for hours. But *at all*. Have you come to this conclusion having worked with it at all? God forbid you're dumping someone who wouldn't dance with you.

*

Here's a poet dancing with it, a playful example for a serious point:

　　Jumbled in one common box
　　Of their dark stupidity,
　　Orchid, swan, and Caesar lie;

> Time that tires of everyone
> Has corroded all the locks,
> Thrown away the key for fun.

A poet of the 'left wing', if one wants to play in that sandpit. Auden's in his lofty stride, lifting rapidly to a realm of types and emblems, fastened with rhyme, aged with meter, always in thought.

> In its cleft the torrent mocks
> Prophets who in days gone by
> Made a profit from each cry,
> Persona grata now with none;
> And a jackass language shocks
> Poets who can only pun.

The second stanza does something intriguing: it runs with an already challenging rhyme-scheme, not only retaining the scheme (ABBCAC, for those who know what that means) but retaining the specific rhymes (*ox, ee/eye, on/un*). That makes the walls start closing in. Soon we're herded into a shrinking space where *only these sounds* can be uttered: an entire society seems to be running in ever smaller circles. Things like that happened in Europe on Auden's watch, then they happened again on ours. A *prophet* is doomed to turn to *profit*, himself but debased. Which Auden then does to, well, himself, as if he *were* a poet 'who can only pun'.

> Silence settles on the clocks;
> Nursing mothers point a sly
> Index finger at a sky,

Crimson in the setting sun;
In the valley of the fox
Gleams the barrel of a gun.

The same scheme, the same rhymes, the same winnowing spiral. The form is remorseless, it will suck up all the rhymes there are – how many can be left in English for *ox*? The pattern suggests the loss of light, the death of choice, the enter-through-trapdoor of the violent worst. And then we see where we were always going, we stumble into the middle of the maze and find idiots at play.

Once we could have made the docks,
Now it is too late to fly;
Once too often you and I
Did what we should not have done;
Round the rampant rugged rocks
Rude and ragged rascals run.

The poem can only have been composed in reverse from that giggling spawn of a tongue-twister. But its alliterating silliness still manages to nail the England I see around me. Or show what societies come to when they only want three things.

*

Rhyme is memorable, mnemonic, a fact our brains filed away before we could walk. But so has alliteration been for us. To understand the full beauty and strangeness of these evolutions, all we have to do is imagine some version of Anglo-Saxon lullaby, softly sung in a warm dark nook near the crackling fire by mother Eldrida to little baby Wulfgar, and going a bit more like this:

Balance baby	on top of tall tree
wind blows westerly	cradle creaking
bough breaks abruptly	cot can't cling
firstborn falling	both bashed, broken

And his tiny eyes are closing. That should do it. Words drawn together against cold. A rhyme might wake the blighter up if he's never known that trick.

*

As we saw – or heard – with meter, it's clear that the shorter the meter the more evident or *present* is the form. With rhyme what matters is the distance between rhymes, so that couplets – two lines together that rhyme – have no interest in concealing their effect, whereas a more complex stanza might separate rhyming words by six, seven, eight lines, in which case the impact of the rhyme is subconscious, kin to musical motif. As Joseph Brodsky writes: 'In poetic thought, the role of the subconscious is played by euphony.'

Half-rhyme ('stone'/'rain') develops in the early years of the 20th century. The principle is the same, a drawing-together of meaning, while softening the *sense* of rhyme, slightly lessening its presence. This multiplies the possibilities about a million-fold, and reminds us that poetry does technically move along sometimes, in theory if not practice.

Some poets say about their work or someone else's that they use a lot of 'internal rhymes' – rhyme that are not at the ends of the lines – when what they mean is that some of the words sound quite like each other. I don't think, by the way, one can 'use enjambment' either – that is, a line flowing without punctuation to the next line. For one thing, as I said before, the line-break *is* punctuation, it's just white instead of black, and for the other, some effects ought to be subconscious in a poet, and I think enjambment and internal rhymes are things you say you're doing but can't help doing. The same goes for anything you call 'assonance'. I imagine I get through a whole shed-load of assonance.

*

Here's what rhyme can do for you if you dance. This is the last section of Shelley's 'Ode to the West Wind'. It's one of the few poems in English written in a form called *terza rima*, the form of Dante's *Divine Comedy*. Watch what the rhymes are up to.

V

Make me thy lyre, even as the forest is:
What if my leaves are falling like its own!
The tumult of thy mighty harmonies

Will take from both a deep, autumnal tone,
Sweet though in sadness. Be thou, Spirit fierce,
My spirit! Be thou me, impetuous one!

Drive my dead thoughts over the universe
Like withered leaves to quicken a new birth!
And, by the incantation of this verse,

Scatter, as from an unextinguished hearth
Ashes and sparks, my words among mankind!
Be through my lips to unawakened earth

The trumpet of a prophecy! O Wind,
If Winter comes, can Spring be far behind?

What they're up to is this. The new rhyme ('own') is born in the second line of every stanza. It recurs in the first line of the next stanza ('tone'), and bids farewell on the third line ('one'). Between the first pair, 'own' and 'tone', a former rhyme ('harmonies') says farewell, and between the second pair, 'tone' and 'one', a new rhyme ('fierce') is born. The pattern repeats for four stanzas until ending at a couplet, which has itself been grown from an earlier rhyme.

This is the creature on the move through life. A new rhyme comes out of the mist, is developed in thought, is left behind. Note how often the middle line – the new rhyme already given force by its position – is also powered by *content*: 'Spirit fierce!' 'a new birth!' 'among mankind!'

Each bright new thought is escorted by a couple of now fading rhymes. If you imagine each rhyme-sound a thick strand of a certain colour, the form would soon resemble DNA, winding and recurring, always changing and never.

Shelley needs it for the sound of inspiration born of miraculous nature.

What does Dante need it for? A journey. A walking creature, walking down, across, up again, guided, time not his own.

Nel mezzo del cammin di nostra vita
mi ritrovai per una selva oscura
ché la diritta via era smarrita.

Ahi quanto a dir qual era è cosa dura
esta selva selvaggia e aspra e forte
che nel pensier rinova la paura!

Tant'è amara che poco è più morte;
ma per trattar del ben ch'i' vi trovai,
dirò de l'altre cose ch'i v'ho scorte...

In his 'Conversation about Dante', the most challenging and sublime essay I know on poetry, Osip Mandelstam wonders:

> how many sandals did Alighieri wear out in the course of his poetic work, wandering about on the goat paths of Italy? The *Inferno* and especially the *Purgatorio* glorify the human gait, the measure and rhythm of walking, the foot and its shape. The step, linked to the breathing and saturated with thought: this Dante understands as the beginning of prosody.

The step, linked to the breathing and saturated with thought.

There isn't so much *terza rima* in English poetry, because it's harder to find trios of full rhymes – in Dante's Italian nearly everything rhymes – but English half-rhyme can get down and do the dirty work. When I needed to tell a story about a man trapped in an infernal circle and seeking his redemption – a poem about the accursed Flying Dutchman which I called *Time's Fool* – I could not see beyond *terza rima*, Dante's mortal coil, spiralling into the distance, or my modified half-rhyming English species:

> When the train stopped I started and woke up.
> Was nowhere, as before, no change in that.
> Nothing new in trundling to a stop
>
> where nothing seemed to call for one. The light
> was winter afternoon, with 'afternoon'
> a term for darkness. In the cold and wet
>
> were trees beside the line, grey evergreen
> unknown by name. And not a soul to hail,
> I said again and with a smile so thin
>
> it died before its life.

I didn't think failure could be sweeter, and still don't.

*

Any form in poetry, be it meter, rhyme, line-break, is a metaphor for creaturely life. It looks to me as if the most durable are those most closely fused to what we are most deeply: organisms that *breathe* and *move* and *have*, who one day horribly learn they can't breathe or move or have forever. – I was sitting on the stairs at night in Hertfordshire, asking my dad 'but *why?*' then my daughter was trotting beside me on a green in Massachusetts, asking me 'but *why?*' There was a time you turned human.

The sound of form in poetry, descended from song, moulded by breath, is the sound of that creature yearning to leave a mark. The meter says *tick-tock*. The rhyme says *remember*. The whiteness says *alone*. The poem forms in space and time. It, at least, can be made to last. It can be what *we* would have created, how *we* would create, had we been We or He or She or I instead of just us.

*

Auden makes the supreme argument for poetic form in general, though he's making it here for meter in particular: 'Blessed be all metrical rules that forbid automatic responses, force us to have second thoughts, free from the fetters of Self.'

Far along on the journey you take with poetic form comes a simple revelation: because poetic form is natural, it resembles freedom. Not absolute freedom, because absolute freedom isn't natural, but all the freedom the creature can gain with his lonely brave black signals in the void.

*

This is all the difference *is* – between form and formlessness, between a governing aesthetic and nothing. You breathe the whiteness, you know lines have to end, you seek out words that fit the music. Your brain, freed from its dull day-job of serving up *the next thing you WOULD think, because you're YOU*, delves deep into the vaults and libraries instead, the dusty sites and attics of all you've known or guessed or heard, sorting and rummaging for a word or phrase that not only *means* right but *sounds* right, *looks* right, *fits* right. Four ways of meaning. Up it comes. Now the poem is not only you, it's you and the language. It's not only you and today, it's you and time.

What's called 'free verse', writing that has broken clear of either the metrical or musical phrase and uses the word 'free' for what it thinks it is now, just isn't up to that. Because nothing is *standing in* for what makes us creatures in a time and place. Whether it's breath, pulse, night and day, footsteps, seasons, nothing is standing in for it.

Nothing is standing in for what keeps us here, holds us. Without the sound of breath, or motion of walking or turning or stretching or sitting or kneeling or touching, without all 'The heart-ache and the thousand natural shocks/That flesh is heir to', without those instruments that have grown out over centuries of speech to *form* the line, the stanza, the breaks, and the beats, all the evasions and allusions and insights you've got in your little quiver won't stop yourself doing what yourself likes doing.

*

I have an ice-breaking exercise I use at this point.

Isabella and Wayne are already sitting one side of the table, Orlando and Mimi on the other. That just happens to be the way I'm pretending it was. It's also raining outside, Mimi looks hungover, and Bella's opening a box of elaborate waxy pastries.

'Once upon a time, all four of you people – I mean *peoples* – lived in harmony on a lush green landmass. Time went by. Like, *a lot* of time went by, and the landmass divided, like Pangaea, into twin continents. Over the ages Bella and Wayne's tribe, on one continent, evolved a language with only two vowels, *a* and *e*. Meanwhile Mimi and Orlando, whose name had mutated first to Ollie, and by now was simply Olli – dwelt on their continent with a tribe whose only vowels were *i, o,* and *u.* The consonants remained the same. They both still possessed *y*. Why? Y. Two roads diverged in a yellow wood. I'll get on with it.'

'Did they not have boats.' 'No Wayne.' 'You'd think they'd have boats.' 'No because the sea on that planet is pure sulphuric acid.' 'Well, professor, that presents all manner of chemical and biological – go on.'

'Okay Wayne, in the end, they invented boats. The queen of the A/E race, called, er, Queen Arabella and the king of the I/O/U folk, um, King Colin, separately decided to sail their fleets to the horizon and see if there was anyone else living on their planet. They met by pure chance on a little deserted island, and then, instead of infecting, enslaving or dismembering each other – because this is kind of a fairytale – they sat down face to face and shared an enormous smorgasbord that stretched for the entire forty miles of this desert rock. Whereupon the A/E race attempted – and the I/O/U folk sought – to understand each other's cultures. What we can see right now in our beloved Room 777 is just one small piece of that legendary picnic. Bella and Olli, Wayne and Mimi, shake hands across the sea.'

*

After some hesitation, some clarification, some eating, we get down to the work of what this is about: *translation*. Because it turns out, amazingly, that these four *peoples* share a common poetic culture – they remember the same poems and songs and stories! Only, these have somewhat mutated over the ages.

For a start, there were so many there from each tribe, it was inevitable that some anniversaries would be celebrated with song on that legendary day. The A/E race's brass band and the I/O/U folk's woodwind group both struck up the same tune, but oh, what contrary strange words rang out in the tropical sunlight –

Happy day here came she!	Your birth hour right now!
Happy day here came she!	Your birth hour right now!
Happy day here came Helga,	Your birth hour right now, Cliff,
Happy day here came she!	Your birth hour right now!

But each embraced the other's song for they recognised the music. Meanwhile their diplomatic, peaceful leaders, Queen Arabella and King Colin, were praised to the skies:

As she's a really sweet lady!	For look, our jolly good top boy!
Yay what a really sweet lady!	O wow, our jolly good top boy!
All cheer that really sweet lady!	Our cool old bountiful top boy!
Hell yes we all agree!	In unison go us!

The A/E race toasted their new friends with real ale, while the I/O/U folk did the honours with gin'n'tonics. Not surprisingly, as the day wore on, things threatened to get slightly out of hand, and you could hear a few chants going up:

Be near and wage war, when ya feel as hard as needed!

Show proximity, do, fight us, if you think your guys got strong!

But peace won the day, peace and Danish pastries, and the sun set on my story.

*

I leave it to you in the graduate bar to work out the originals of these stanzas my little class came up with:

1   Hey, met an aged seafarer,
    Makes me halt, lets them by.
    'Hey beardy, mad-eyed elder,
    Why d'ya halt and hassle me?'
               [from 'The Endless Verses Read By the Aged
               Seafarer That Made Me Late At The
               Party Held When Angela Fackenham-Tray and
               Edward Heffenden-Dedley Were Wed']

2   Turning, turning, in this big-growing ring,
    High bird will know no sound of who owns him.
    Things go to shit, stuff will not truly hold.
    Do stuff you just itch to do! is cry of my world.
         [from 'Slouching to Holy Towns']

3   You do not do, you do not do,
    Not now, brown clog
    In which I got stuck, my foot stuck
    For thirty springs, poor, thin,
    Not risking gulp, nor risking sniff.
         [from 'Pops']

4   They screw ya, ma and pa, hell yes.
    Maybe can't help themselves. Beats me.
    Bequeath ya all the mess they made
    And add the extra garbage free.
         ['That Be The Verse']

*

Actors can learn thousands of lines because they learned hundreds of lines. They can learn hundreds of lines because they learned dozens of lines. Exercise is exercise. One January the first I started memorizing a poem every day and it just got easier each time. I stopped by the end of March because I got both lazy and busy in ways other poets would recognize, but I still know a good many. Do something every day and that interior road becomes clear, clean, swept, maintained.

If it works for memorization, there's no reason it shouldn't work for word-substitution, for hunting in the word-hoard. Translation can get you there too, but the Vowel Game is good for students both on their guard and off it. I'm afraid to say it's a team-bonding thing, but a team-bonding thing it is.

And I've not a clue what lights go on or bells go off in the brain, I just think it's healthy for a poet to depart from himself, leave herself behind, to light strings of cerebral lanterns, streaming away in all directions, away from the brilliant boring wine-and-cheese Do Of The Ego, away from what you're bound to say next because you always say it next, lamps marching away out of reach, over the hills, into the darkness –

> *What means what I want to say yet sounds like it needs to sound?*
> *And looks like it needs to look...*
> *And means what I also want...*
>
> *This does!*
>
> *So where does that leave me now?*

– In unrivalled brimming black, with words you didn't expect, echoes you couldn't foresee, matter you never chose, resonances that crept up around you to wait for your next move.

This is not you the writer of poems. This is you the poem, this is you in the language. Not you, you in the language. Not you today, you in time.

The thing you are, at that point, simply knows more than you do. To say the least, only *it* can get you out of there.

*

Orlando keeps up the vowel thing for ages in the graduate pub that evening, and Bella finds it easier and easier technically, while finding it harder and harder to bother. Wayne, working with his iBall at the next table, has already explained that what we just had was an Oulipo class.

'I don't think our professor knows that,' he says, then he's off to his Computer-Gaming Module in Jobs 109, where they say he's trying to develop *Poetry Workshop Wipeout* to sell to the folk who make *The Sims*.

'Perhaps less clear as regards why,' Ollie goes when Wayne's gone and they're together.

'Mm-hm,' says Isabella, using no vowels because she suddenly can't remember which ones she can use or not use. Or what Ollie's talking about. He's grinning at her like he does.

'Why class – takes shape – class takes, exactly.'

Bella dully remembers he said he'd married into the A/E tribe and had forsaken his old ways or something.

'Yep,' she says after thought, stirring her drink anti-clockwise.

'*e!* Can't say *yep*,' says Ollie, 'A/E! That's the past!'

'Nope,' says Bella, stirring it clockwise.

'Can't say that! That has – an *e* at the end!'

'Nop,' says Isabella, finishing her drink. She better get home, she wants to watch that murder thing she likes.

'Catch it on iPlayer,' Ollie suggests, obviously.

'You mean ePlayer or aPlayer,' she points out, summoning one last drop of wit from the smoking carcass of my class all those hours ago.

When Bella is gone, and Ollie stumbles into Mimi much later in some crowded nightspot, and she goes 'Oi *Orlando* let's me and you get wrecked', his mind is so distracted with how many vowel-mistakes she's made ('What gang these days, yay female classmate?) that he fails to grasp what she was actually asking of him and by the time he got it she'd met some strangers she played poker with till morning.

˷

Space

I AM GOING TO venture to make some observations based on my own experience, which will lead me to comment on my intentions, failures, and partial successes, in my own plays. I do this in the belief that any explorer or experimenter in new territory may, by putting on record a kind of journal of his explorations, say something of use to those who follow him into the same regions and who will perhaps go further.

*

T. S. Eliot said that to me in November 1950, in the form of the First Theodore Spencer Memorial Lecture at Harvard University. No I wasn't there, I couldn't make it, but still he said it to me. He was explicitly imagining a poet of the future writing plays in verse; he was giving advice, encouragement, words of warning. There's no sign of the hieratic lectern-bothering Eliot in this piece: this is the log of a craftsman, humble and thoughtful: 'Well, I had made some progress in learning how to write the first act of a play', he says cautiously, then claims of *The Cocktail Party* (perhaps debatably) that he avoided 'poetry which could not stand the test of strict dramatic utility.' He tries to learn from experience: 'no chorus, and no ghosts', and rather relishes his past discomforts, as when he recalls trying to make dramatically convincing the Furies in *The Family Reunion*:

> We tried every possible manner of presenting them. We
> put them on the stage, and they looked like uninvited guests

who had strayed in from a fancy-dress ball. We concealed
them behind gauze, and they suggested a still out of a Walt
Disney film. We made them dimmer, and they looked like
shrubbery just outside the window.

This is the poet stuck in the chaos of theatre, as three girls in
crinkly Fury costumes giggle in an empty row, the ASM turns
the air blue and the lighting man tries just one more thing; this
is the director asking a poet what he means then telling him
what he really means, the whole mess of scripts and sets and
coffee and revisions, as the isolated maker sweeps a red biro like
Excalibur through a lovely line he thought of when out walking,
and sighs and contemplates the spot-lit rubble of what's left.

So consider Eliot's generous sentiment received in the right
spirit. I'm also, if nothing else, a 'writer who has worked for years'
and who has 'achieved some success...in writing other kinds of
verse' – by which Eliot meant lyric or comic or narrative poetry
as opposed to verse plays – and who has spent most of his writing
life trying to write verse that can live on stage. And, though
Eliot doesn't say this in the Harvard lecture, we do also have
the following in common: the taking of a draught of a certain
dizzying cocktail: high praise and low derision, sometimes for
the same play, often for the same performance – and therefore
cancelling out to little but a wry perspective on the business, a
genial but total contempt for those munching bystanders who
risk nothing, and a brand new blank slate.

*

What I know about the making of a play, the arcs, the
aesthetics, the character-journeys – I was going to say that

would take a different book. But it wouldn't, it would scarcely fill a page, what very little I'm sure about on that score. You learn you know nothing, my teacher said once, and that's where I'm headed. This is a poet's book and a book about poets, so its 'Space' chapter is primarily about utterance, about *verse on stage*, about how a verse-line relates to character, situation, style. The blackness and the whiteness in this chapter are always – whatever else they are – speech and silence. The chapter is about what poets think they can bring to the theatre (which they're wrong about) and what they actually can (which I hope one day they will.)

I'm not alone among the poets of today in having ventured into theatre, but I'm close to alone, and sometimes I wonder why. I've told you all I know, that poetry is creaturely, that creatures move in space and time and collide with others gladly or sadly or avoid them altogether. There is *nothing* you can write about speaking or silence that pertains only to poetry. If you can compose lines that breathe, an actor can say them. In fact, there is no single thing a young poet can do that is more useful than letting his or her lines pass through the mind and lungs and throat and lips of a well-trained actor. If you know your blackness and whiteness, your line-form and line-break, your meters and measures, how to ride and not be ridden, then you're in – literally – good shape. You can deploy the breath and silence in ways prose writers (99% of playwrights) never learn to. All you need beyond that are good stories, and you can swipe them from anywhere, as Shakespeare did. So there's nothing to stop poets writing and staging plays but fear and economics.

And if you're writing poetry you'll have put those two in their place years ago.

*

Some things are so manifestly true they can't be budged. So in time they get called clichés or freeze to jokes, but they stay true. So it is with the actor asking plaintively: *What's my motivation?* But this is no different to my interrogation of the poem: why is that word there? Why that line-break? Why that metaphor? For what reason does obscurity take precedence over clarity? Or saying take precedence over silence? The trained actor is a first responder to language. He or she receives the language before the director, the audience, the critics. The approbation or otherwise of good actors is more telling than notes or applause or catcalls or cheers or tears or reviews, because whatever shape the story's in, the production, the event, at least it's clear the characters are creatures, and without that one has nothing.

In the chapter called 'White' we cast great song-lyrics into the *blancheur* and they shrivelled like film in fire. You bring bad lines to good actors and you can meet that devouring force at first hand, as they respectfully (usually) and seriously (always) say *I don't think I'd say this. I wouldn't say that to her now she's said that to me. He's standing too far away for me to say it like that. My character wouldn't listen any longer to her. I don't think I'd say anything at all.*

This last one happened lately. In my play *After Troy*, the desolate Hecuba confronts the tribal chief Mestor whom she thought was her friend, but whom she now knows has murdered her youngest son. Mestor doesn't know she knows. I wrote numb, twisted, strangled lines for her in her masked rage and grief, but the actress, having gone where the words took her, came back from that dark place, found me in the pub after rehearsal and said *I don't think she'd say a word.* When actors ask for *fewer* lines you know they're dead serious.

And if you're new to this, and you think you're the only maker here, you try to stare that down: it's not your character it's mine, so I know, so there. But you don't, because, poet, now that the words are passing through the souls of actors, *you're* new to your play too, and someone who has trained about a thousand times harder than you and in the company of some of the best English ever written is telling you what she knows, what he knows, what their bodies know about English. Know as much as they do; only then you can stare them down. I cut all Hecuba's lines in the scene and we got a silence of absolute ferocity as she stared at Mestor gibbering his bullshit. Then she gouged his eyes out.

Actors are hungry for verse *because* it's creaturely. They know when it's true or false. They hear it in the gut, the lungs, the windpipe. Lines of the classics are creaturely, which we know because they're still speaking to us, so the best actors have travelled far beyond that clump of shrubbery from which dull voices ever burble *verse isn't natural, meter's not authentic, rhyme isn't real.* Perhaps people who think that way somehow believe that four hundred years ago we really did speak in high pentameters and complex metaphors dreamed up on the spot, or rhyme as we left the room, leaving some vagabonds and clowns to clatter in and swap incomprehensible prose riddles while we powdered our noses.

*

When I was about fifteen I first encountered this.

Regan.   Witness the world, that I create thee here
        My lord and master.
Goneril.   Mean you to enjoy him?
Albany.   The let-alone lies not in your good will.
Edmund. Nor in thine, lord.
Albany.   Half-blooded fellow, yes.
Regan.   Let the drum strike, and prove my title thine.
Albany.   Stay yet; hear reason. Edmund I arrest thee
        On capital treason; and, in thy attaint,
        This gilded serpent.

These lines of *King Lear* set things ablaze for me. Not a great tragic monologue, not a deep rumination, not the knockabout comedy, not the songs, not the spells, not *poetry* as I understood it at that age, but this nasty spat between two poisonous sisters, a malevolent schemer, and a decent sort getting the big picture too late. I was staggered by the sense of multitude, of creatures rubbing and bristling past each other. Goneril and Regan both want Edmund, but only Regan can have him, because she's been widowed whereas Goneril's stuck with Albany. She thinks he's useless, he's figured out she's vile, he despises the 'halfblood' Edmund, Edmund thinks he's a weed, Albany pulls rank. Mostly they'll be dead soon. Time is dragging them bodily behind it. The meter is the world turning.

One thing I found so exhilarating here was unlocked for me by the words of a poet, Yeats, one of the few to have written compelling drama in the last century. (I mean, I venerate Frost and Auden to the moon as poets but in their theatre writing they never get themselves off the stage.) Here's Yeats:

> The Shakespearian Drama gets the emotion of multitude out of the subplot which copies the main plot, much as a shadow upon the wall copies one's body in the firelight...Lear's shadow is in Gloster, who also has ungrateful children, and the mind goes on imagining other shadows, shadow beyond shadow until it has pictured the world.

I craved that sense of multitude in my writing, and it drew me to the theatre.

*

The meter is the world turning. Look at this again:

Edmund. Nor in thine, lord.
Albany.　　　　　　Half-blooded fellow, yes.

These men hate each other. But they share this line.

> Nor in thine, lord. Half-blooded fellow, yes.
> Nor in thine lord half blooded fellow yes.

The textual indent before Albany's words is misleading – there's no space there at all, it merely indicates it's a half-line. What it's actually saying is *leave no gap*. You can outright *kill* Shakespeare – let alone kill me and I have died many times – by pausing in those half-lines.

Imagine this quarrel scene without shared lines, without versification.

Regan. Witness the world, that I create thee here my lord and master.

Goneril. Mean you to enjoy him?

Albany. The let-alone lies not in your good will.

Edmund. Nor in thine, lord.

Albany. Half-blooded fellow, yes.

Regan. Let the drum strike, and prove my title thine.

Albany. Stay yet; hear reason. Edmund I arrest thee on capital treason;
and, in thy attaint, this gilded serpent.

Hideous. Bogged down. And not composed like that. Verse playwrights write like composers: the lay-out is musical score. When actors don't understand that, or aren't interested in anyone *else's* Method, they mix the black and white like amateurs and wonder who turned their lines grey.

The form fuses creatures, bonds them, shackles them. Albany's 'Half' jumps in indignantly, can't even wait for one unstressed instant. The meter is the world turning, day passing, grass growing. Silence costs too much to these beating hearts. Think of the price of *nothing* in Shakespeare: Cordelia's silence when Lear asks her to compete publicly for his love is what sets the disaster in train. Again, something and nothing, blackness and whiteness, showing their true colours.

Cordelia will be silent again in time:

> Why should a dog, a horse, a rat have life,
> And thou no breath at all? Thou'lt come no more,
> Never, never, never, never, never.

These are effects of form, and in this playwright effects of *pentameter*: the absent line, or the broken, the split but essentially *whole,* length-of-a-breath line, expressing life as lived by fractured creatures drawn together at the feet of passing time.

Here, by contrast, to lift the dark mood, are rhymed pentameters expressing ecstasy:

Romeo.	If I profane with my unworthiest hand
	This holy shrine, the gentle fine is this:
	My lips, two blushing pilgrims, ready stand
	To smooth that rough touch with a tender kiss.
Juliet.	Good pilgrim, you do wrong your hand too much,
	Which mannerly devotion shows in this;
	For saints have hands that pilgrims' hands do touch,
	And palm to palm is holy palmers' kiss.
Romeo.	Have not saints lips, and holy palmers too?
Juliet.	Ay, pilgrim, lips that they must use in prayer.
Romeo.	O, then, dear saint, let lips do what hands do;
	They pray, grant thou, lest faith turn to despair.
Juliet.	Saints do not move, though grant for prayers' sake.
Romeo.	Then move not, while my prayer's effect I take.

Sonnet? Yes. Over? No. Exception to the rule, in sonnets as in certain other things that two can share: if you're making the thing together you can go on as long as you damn well please.

Romeo.	Thus from my lips, by yours, my sin is purged.
Juliet.	Then have my lips the sin that they have took.
Romeo.	Sin from thy lips? O trespass sweetly urged!
	Give me my sin again.
Juliet.	– You kiss by the book.

Or as long as you physically can. Notice how, as soon as the sonnet-length has passed and the clock struck fourteen, all they can talk about is lips. Try speaking those lines with another and only one thing's going to happen. No need to thank me. Effects of form.

*

Two hundred years or so earlier, a nameless playwright depicts the Crucifixion as part of the York Mystery Cycle. Four Roman soldiers nail Christ to a cross. The town's nail-makers – 'pinners' – have been cast to do this, just as early this morning the water-drawers gave their Noah's Flood and the goldsmiths stepped in about lunchtime for the Adoration of the Magi. The play has 300 lines, of which a mere twelve are Christ's, addressing His Father. The rest of the action consists of these four professional pinners talking as they work, taking *real time* to measure and cut two lengths of wood, hammer them together properly, then pretend to nail a man to it:

1st Soldier. Sir knyghtis, saie, howe wirke we nowe?
2nd Soldier. Yis, certis, I hope I holde this hande.
3rd Soldier. And to the boore I have it brought
         Full boxumly with-outen bande.
4th Soldier. Strike on than harde, for hym the boght.
1st Soldier. Yis, here is a stubbe will stiffely stande;
         Thurgh bones and senous it schall be soght.
         This werke is well, I will warande.

Effects of form: the work cannot stop, the talk cannot stop. The meter turns the earth beneath four men doing what they do with their lives. Rhyme and alliteration combine in rhythmic four-beat lines: whatever else it is in the great scheme of things, it's a work-song. *Primarily* it's a work-song. It takes the time it takes. And for this reason, regardless of the highly-wrought and artificial form this play takes, the writer is known to us now as 'The York Realist'.

*

Realism, naturalism now? Many talented playwrights make fine work out of prose, and some – a very much smaller group – have the skill to make the voices of their creatures actually sound different from one another. It's alarming how many don't. But verse ought to *do this better than prose.* As with so-called 'free' verse, voices will, without the pressure of line-end or meter or rhyme or pattern, say exactly what their maker wants them to say next, which is why so many rather successful playwrights write characters who sound the same as each other, while either agreeing with the playwright in an attractive way or disagreeing like fools. Mind, if the characters combine to voice a world-view the crowd is happy with, you have instant genius in the house, which we're lucky to have quite often.

In a poem, you can render – in fact you *must* render – a coherent and consistent voice that doesn't have to be you – in fact *isn't* you, for you are a creature, and not black ink or pixels. If you extend that principle to characters in a play – this character knows x much and says things in a y way, while this one knows z much and says things in a w way – verse can heighten the effect, because you are putting into action manifold ways a particular creature works with the white and black, the nothing and something, the warmth of the spotlit blaze – the line's length – and the horror of the shadowy soundless wings –

the line's end. What are my words, my ambit? How wide is the ring around me that contains what I know or what I believe? What does it mean to me to be here in the light? What does it cost to speak? What does it cost to be silent? To be gone? Verse is, in comparison with prose, a measurable and governable way of creating distinctions in voice.

And how to make your creatures? Well, the following applies to any play, a poet's or not, but is so delightful and insightful a passage it deserves an appearance. It's Yeats again, at first quoting the poet and playwright Goethe:

> 'We do the people of history the honour of naming
> them after the creations of our own minds.'...One day, as
> [Shakespeare] sat over Holinshed's *History of England*, he
> persuaded himself that Richard the Second, with his French
> culture, 'his too great friendliness to his friends,' his beauty
> of mind, and his fall before dry, repelling Bolingbroke,
> would be a good image for an accustomed mood of fanciful,
> impractical lyricism in his own mind.

If you're a poet, now you've made another. You awaken a north in you, a south or east or west or any magpie mess of these. You tilt the mind that way. In my work I sometimes feel myself physically changing posture as I write for character *x* (sit upright and frown), character *y* (slouch and smile), character *z* (slouch and frown). They are not I. Find them in the language.

What is the black utterance to *Richard II in particular*, and what is the white silence? How many words does he have, and how does he love them? He will grow away from you, and so will she, and they, and it, and all the creatures you made, because they were born not only of you, but of your will in love with your language, and shored against silence. They are wrought by pressures of form and story into unique identity.

*

The Elizabethan and Jacobean theatres, for fascinating reasons that mattered earlier but don't right now, arrived at the pentameter as the dominant mode of speech. This became the *form* of expressed life. This line became the sound of breathing creatures passing through moments of time. It is no less natural, and no more arbitrary, than the following conventions of 'prose' theatre, all the way to the most 'naturalistic' – that is, all the way to television – that characters speak in turn; that everything they say is clear to the audience; that everything they say is either clear to each other, or significantly obscure; that everything they say *matters to the story.* These are conventions. If you want to see some interesting first steps away from some of those, you could do worse than look at *The Wire.*

*

Journeys start in ignorance, and for several years, as I started corralling my friends and family into outdoor spectaculars in a space called my garden, I couldn't really see beyond lyricism. I believed that what a poet could bring to the theatre was beauty, heights and flights, a late 20th-century shot at Marlowe's mighty line. But this narrow concept of beauty, poetic or lyric if you like, is precisely what poets should dump at the stage door.

Eliot could have told me this in 1950, had I been listening: 'the self-education of a poet trying to write for the theatre seems to require a long period of disciplining his poetry, and putting it, so to speak, on a very thin diet in order to adapt it to the needs of the drama...'

For his plays may seem less than his poetry or his criticism, but in the macabre fragments of *Sweeney Agonistes* you can see tiny seeds and nuts of Beckett, Pinter, *Monty Python,* Caryl Churchill, Bryony Lavery:

SWARTS: These fellows always get pinched in the end.

SNOW: Excuse me, they don't all get pinched in the end.

   What about them bones on Epsom Heath?

   I seen that in the papers

   You seen that in the papers

   They *don't* all get pinched in the end.

DORIS: A woman runs a terrible risk.

SNOW: Let Mr Sweeney continue his story.

SWEENEY: This one didn't get pinched in the end

   But that's another story too.

   This went on for a couple of months

   Nobody came

   And nobody went

   But he took in the milk and he paid the rent.

SWARTS: What did he do? All that time, what did he do?

SWEENEY: What did he do! what did he do?

   That don't apply.

   Talk to live men about what they do.

   He used to come and see me sometimes

   I'd give him a drink and cheer him up.

DORIS: Cheer him up?

DUSTY: Cheer him up?
SWEENER: Well here again that don't apply
                But I've gotta use words when I talk to you.

*

Without a playwright's instincts a poet can bring nothing at all to the space. But the poet who *mines, sounds, cultivates* the black and white of the page to their fullest extent is learning much the same as what a dramatist learns about presence and absence, time flying or grinding by, nearness to a heartbeat, distance from any, and the helpless tendency of ordinary life to sigh, put down its tools, and give in to story.

*

A great Irish poet once chuckled to me that he hadn't done much work in theatre because he found it tough to get people on or off the stage. I thought that was a profound understanding and equipped him perfectly. Poet or playwright, you embrace the reality of the artifice: entrances, exits, stories, stanzas, rhymes, lines, *writing at all.* Whatever the story you're telling, something in the make-up of this character wants to get into the light, be lit by the blaze, be heard, be remembered. Here's Yeats in *Lapis Lazuli*:

> All perform their tragic play,
> There struts Hamlet, there is Lear,
> That's Ophelia, that Cordelia;
> Yet they, should the last scene be there,
> The great stage curtain about to drop,
> If worthy their prominent part in the play,

Do not break up their lines to weep.
They know that Hamlet and Lear are gay;
Gaiety transfiguring all that dread.

*

When a play of mine is coming on, the only thing I say to – or rather, beg of – the publicity people is '*Please* don't say it's in verse.' Verse drama, while it goes by that name, wears that costume, looks like a fool in the marketplace. But he's more Lear's Fool than yours, that verse drama, because those plays are everywhere. Our national theatre is Shakespeare Etc. By and large, the drama critics of our marketplace wait for two things only: to see the next famous lovely face have A Crack At The Bard – an Olympics we're truly trapped inside forever – or to cry out that someone, that young new Etc, 'makes Sarah Kane look like Alan Ayckbourn.' That is, to be the meerkat who fixed his little eyes longest on the future.

What if theatre doesn't come from the future?

*

In his 1950 lecture, Eliot asserts that audiences should be made to hear verse 'from people dressed like ourselves, living in houses and apartments like ours, and using telephones and motorcars and radio sets.' And bullet-trains and iPads and facebook, and of course he's right. But as long as audiences associate verse with a golden, heightened, improbable past, and poets lug the glittering cart of their *poetry* into the space with them, and new playwrights reflexively associate the present with ugliness and fracture and the false real of TV, and critics keep a spellbound guard on the Great or a frozen watch for the New, this forward shift can never be made.

The Modernists brought the bric-a-brac of the Now into poetry: that's half the work accomplished; we're at home in detritus. For the other half, the undone half, the unessayed half, *a way to sound it*, let's go back to Edward Thomas.

> The sorrow of true love is a great sorrow.
> So have I heard, and do in part believe it.

Or do I mean Robert Frost?

> Something there is that doesn't love a wall.
> So have I heard, and do in part believe it.

Actually it's neither.

Marcellus.	It faded on the crowing of the cock.
	Some say that ever 'gainst that season comes
	Wherein our Saviour's birth is celebrated,
	This bird of dawning singeth all night long;
	And then, they say, no spirit dare stir abroad,
	The nights are wholesome, then no planets strike,
	No fairy takes, nor witch hath power to charm,
	So hallowed and so gracious is that time.
Horatio.	So have I heard, and do in part believe it.

This was Robert Frost's favourite line in all Shakespeare. And of course it wouldn't jar in a poem by Frost or Thomas. It's a passing of time – an effect of form – and, as Mandelstam said of the lines of Dante, *saturated with thought*. At first glance the line looks almost colourless, featureless, one a fool would cut for sure, but to me it's contemporary poetry, and it will one day bring us back into theatre, because it tells us the pentameter can breathe right now as it breathed back then.

*

The liberal, educated Horatio lets the blue-collar soldier run on with his superstitions, his 'some say' and his 'they say', and Horatio would, to the ears of Marcellus and the other watchmen, appear to concur. But he probably doesn't concur at all: out of politeness he chimes with the soldier but can't resist the softly qualifying 'in part'. He has of course seen the Ghost at this point, but is perhaps processing the sight, rummaging for a rational cause. He's not ready to shatter his reasonable world-view any further by embracing the superstitions of every man jack. The point is that the pentameter *gives him* that 'in part'. It's the sound of the mind passing through the moment and *helplessly* revealing character: 'So have I heard, and do in part believe it.'

And here's some actual Thomas, beating a path to contemporary dramatic utterance, stretched over heartbeat, helpless in the face of light, verse as a mattering breath:

'Have you been out?' 'No.' 'And don't want to, perhaps?'
If I could only come back again, I should.
I could spare an arm. I shouldn't want to lose
A leg. If I should lose my head, why, so,
I should want nothing more... Have many gone
From here?' 'Yes.' 'Many lost?' 'Yes: a good few.
Only two teams work on the farm this year.
One of my mates is dead. The second day

> In France they killed him. It was back in March,
> The very night of the blizzard, too. Now if
> He had stayed here we should have moved that tree.'
> 'And I should not have sat here. Everything
> Would have been different, for it would have been
> Another world.' 'Ay, and a better, though
> If we could see all all might seem good...'

If the meter is a constant, and I mean the bars *behind* the music, I mean the ghost of the metronome, then character can be infinitely played against it, across it, along it. For example, characters like Horatio, Hamlet, Beatrice, Hal, Rosalind or Prospero have wide vocabularies, rich word-hoards, and the lines go by at the pace of thought. Comic or rustic characters have great vocabularies too – we are talking about Shakespeare, after all, who either won't or *can't* write the inarticulate, only sometimes the tongue-tied – but those folks tend to tumble into prose.

Whereas, *whereas* – what a constantly shadowing meter can do is *reveal* the voice of the helpless-inarticulate, by sounding its inability to move at the pace of the lines, sounding its *not-knowing* against the relentless turning of the earth. Samuel Beckett and his inheritors bring some of this – the sounding of the helpless-inarticulate – but they don't bring it in verse. And that's what I'm thinking of, and what I continue to try for: verse, the contemporary pentameter preserved and deepened in the 20th century by the likes of Thomas and Frost and those who follow, the sound of light arriving in the moment, growing at creaturely rate into thought or feeling, the earth turning beneath the feet of the happy, the sad, the virtuous and vile, the rude, the polite, the bright and the clueless, the ruined, the rewarded, the blessed and the doomed.

So, in the spirit of T.S. Eliot and all poets who have ventured or will venture into the dazzling bright and awful dark of theatre, I pass on what I did, what I found, what I learned. I stand beside it; I stand by it. It's been a lonely row to hoe, so, to echo the master who began this chapter, I'll call out across the fields in all seven directions: north, south, east, west, up, down, and after.

*

In *After Troy,* the imprisoned Andromache is glad to see the courteous Talthybius, who will take her to visit her little boy Astyanax in the children's prison. But the Greeks have hurled the child to his death already, and left the aghast civil-servant to tell her. In the end he doesn't need to.

Andromache.	You can – take me to see my son.
	Your face makes your dead parchment look rich
	with life. Why am I sitting down,
	I am sitting down
	not standing when you say that, not, not
	leaping in the air. I am someone else
	who is sitting down. Let us – try again. I ask you:
	may I see my son now?
Talthybius.	Yes – you may – see him.
Andromache.	Look at me, still here. The dream comes true
	and I sit and pass the time. But I can see him?
	Will he be glad to see me?
	Astyanax? *That's my Astyanax!*

Remember when I screamed that? You took me,
didn't you, you said *escort the widow*
escort the widow of Hector to the camp
of the infants to be with her son. To see him.
You took away the blindfold. *Can you see him?*
And I screamed and ran to him, did I not scream?
I ran through all the children all the babies
and picked him up and flew him round and round
like the sun around the world! You were smiling.
You may not think so now but you were smiling.
So then, at at at that time,
you learned which one he was. I was your teacher,
and you you you you learned – you – didn't know
which one he was so you said I could see him.
So then, you knew.

Talthybius.	Good lady,

I was told to bring you to him.

Andromache.	And you did do,

you you you did do – then you you you knew
which which which child he was and I can see him
I can see him now.

Talthybius.	You can see him, my dear lady

Andromache.

Andromache.	Good lady dear lady

you can see him you can see him, you can
tell me where he is you you can tell me
which which which one. Good lady good lady

*

The next and last chapter of my book on poetry is called, of course, 'Time'.

I was going to call it 'Poem', as I wanted to pay tribute to poet-teachers from Coleridge to John Hollander, who've illustrated forms by showing them in use. But it isn't a poem, it's not inscribed on whiteness, it can't breathe independently of all that's gone before. Really it's a cacophony, but it should be, there being, as I said at the outset, as many outlooks on poetry as there are readers of it. It's a pandemonium, all the little creatures let loose in daylight. It's my workshop on a holiday, its doors all open.

And I know our culture is book-ended – either side of where knowledge ends – by folks who believe anything and folks who believe nothing. In between are many who believe what they read for sure, as long as it's in prose. Many of these write poetry, oddly, but go to prose to learn about it. If they want to drop out here, I won't fail them. When I first taught in New York I was interested to see that while my students' examination of me ran to three printed pages of thoroughly candid observations, my judgment of them was confined to a choice of two pictograms: P (they showed up, semi-circle complete) or F (they didn't, semi-circle broken.)

But I hope you show up to this, to the Wedding Feast, and leave the poor Wedding-Guest behind to hear the Ancient Mariner all day and all night forever, I hope you'll come with the evolutionary psychologists and me to the Wedding Feast, where – what can we see?

A garden (we can hunt) beside a house with many rooms (we can hide), a great banquet being prepared (we can eat) and a thousand bottles of wine (we can escape). We see people (we can laugh, learn, love, fight), we see the sun high in the sky (we have all the time in the world) and we see a dance-floor (we will prove we're fit for anything). All in all we like what we see. A wedding-day but not yours: time at its brightest, sharpest, and strangest.

So I hope you'll come with me, and the evolutionary psychologists, and Ned Stowey, and Bill Porlock, and Byron and Browning and Emily Dickinson, and T. S. Eliot's three giggling Furies, and some boring professors I met along the way, and Dante's Nimrod and Yeats's Wandering Aengus, and a Riddler from long ago and a Taxpayer from now, and Helga with her a/e language, Cliff with his i/o/u, and my imaginary and imaginative students Ollie and Bella and Mimi and Wayne, and of course the dear radiant blushing bride Miss Angela Fackenham-Tray and her hungover husband-to-be, good old Edward Heffenden-Dedley, and I hope you'll accept the invitation in the spirit in which I give it. Frost wrote that poetry 'begins in delight and ends in wisdom'. I think the wise poet is always beginning, always – where the black meets the white – delighted to be *at it*, and the rest I'm more than happy to render up to Time.

~

Time

There was a ship – we don't have time for this!
cries Stowey to two mates, the one who gasps
and seconds that – *No dice!* – and the one who stays,
who didn't have time either,

    but stayed,

dwindled as they left him on the footpath
with the ragged clutching soul. *Catch us up eh!*
Ned yells in earshot – neither figure turned
so the two pass on delighted

    to a garden.

Under the threaded arch they move in bliss,
Bill Porlock and Ned Stowey, to the feast
set out so early in the noonday sun
with all of you, how ever

    should time

dare to pass? O over the lawns they stroll
to everything they wished. They don't say so
but they think they'll find love here today, does Bill,
does Ned, and soon they do

    say so.

TIME

*

Angela Fackenham-Tray
Is getting married today
In fact has been married an hour,
Is posing in a traditional bower

Beheld by family, bestest friends
All peek-a-boo behind a lens
But, when not freezing for a snap,
Our bride is glowering at this chap

Who just an hour ago she vowed
To have and hold for keeps, out loud.
She made her pledge, he made his oath.
(Thank Christ she thought to write them both.)

Me happy, yay, my day, all sweet,
We're wed, new pals, eat what we eat!
Patter? Small feet? Faraway!
Be self, express, be free, wahay!

Angela Fackenham-Tray
Got married again today
In fact was married two hours and a quarter
When heard to hiss *Bloody drink some water.*

*

If the beautiful seating plan had eyes, it would see
Bill Porlock taking his glasses off to see
if chance has placed him next to his old friend Ned
and no one else because apart from his school-friend Ned –
and his other school-friend who for some strange reason stopped
to hear that sea-dog fellow, the one who stopped
and pestered them – apart from those two shipmates
Bill doesn't know a soul. 'Result! Two shipmates
together! Table 40! Solid!' But Ned's
not listening, Ned's
gazing off at this tall girl in a dress
of green, what a day, O girl who chose a green dress,
who frowned in her flowery things in the face of her wardrobe,
reached with a sigh deep into her Narnia wardrobe,
selected a lipstick before Ned saw her,
rode in a car before Ned saw her,
lived half her life!
well, half her young life,
now shields her eyes, and he's saying to no one at all
'I hope that honey in green's on our table...' it's all
he hopes. And Bill Porlock, listening, having nobody
else to listen to, wiping his glasses, nobody
else's name to locate on the crayoned plan
says 'Tell me her name and I'll check on this crayoned Plan,
shipmate.' And Ned says reasonably 'I don't know
her sodding name, do I. All I know...'
Bill Porlock waits and wonders what it is,
but it's nothing. Bill squints at the Plan and says 'If her name is
Lucy Gray, Eldrida Half-Dane,

that's a funny old name that, Half-Dane,
Group-Captain Henry Jones –
Group-Captain Henry Jones
is unlikely to be her name – if it's Bella Croft
then yes, she's on our table, BELLA CROFT,'
Bill suddenly says too loud like an utter moron
and the tall girl looks and Ned says 'Bill you tosser.'

*

'And, ninthly,' said the gentleman to Orlando,
as they started on their starters, and already
soup was adventuring down the weathered jawbone,
'how can one *learn* to write, is that a thing
one can be *taught*?' Ollie began to say 'I – '
'Well *I* should have thought,' said the elderly man with the elbow
at his other flank, '*I* should have thought that if one,
were to be termed, for the sake of argument, a "creative"
"writer", one ought really to have invented
an entirely, new, colour!' Both those fellows
rocked and streamed with laughter, 'That's how they do it
in that village in the Fens!' 'That's how they do it
in that factory in the Cotswolds!' Orlando:
'what you mean Cambridge and Oxford.' 'Yes, and tenthly...'

*

The happiest day of their lives is the last ever.

'Is it rude like the other one?' enquires a taxpayer,
'because also I don't see how a key remotely

resembles a cock.' The riddler drains his cider
at his fifty-thousandth wedding. 'It's not rude,'
he shrugs. A reticent lady dressed in white
who's not said a word now suddenly says 'What – is Rude –
about – a Cock?' and Table 18 goes quiet.
The happiest day of their lives is the last ever.

Wayne is working it out, he's in primary colours
from head to toe and working it out on his iBall,
but still he has time to confide to the quiet lady
considerately 'It's not cock as in poultry, my friend,
and I'm taking a poultry workshop, so I know,'
as a cloud moves off and they realise it was cloudy
– The happiest day of their lives is the last ever –

now it's sunny and dust is dancing in a slant
at the face of the lady in white, who now says: 'Yes –
Cock as in – your Knob – sir.' And Wayne splutters
fish-bits over his fish. The taxpayer checks
his Blackberry and the riddler reaches for pepper.
The happiest day of their lives is the last ever.

A girl and a boy have been whispering close together
since they sat down, they had never met, but they share
a birthday and have been doing nothing else
but sharing since, now they share dessert: 'Sweet day
began and here we stay!' says Helga. Cliff
simply nods: 'You look, I look, it's just tops
to know you, Hilgi...' 'Helga.' 'Hylgo...' 'Whatever.'
'Fiancés,' Wayne calls out twelve seconds later.
The happiest day of their lives is the last ever.

TIME

*

Speech. Speech.
        Me daughter dear,
Proud as sterling, shedded a tear,
Day's the day, the gang's all here.

Speech. Speech.
        We? She?
Beauty means we're meant to be?
Wake me, shake me, pity me!

Speech. Speech.
        Get on with it.
Done your bit. I'll do my bit.
You, me, gatepost. Chap's a shit.

*

Ned is defacing the card that says NED STOWEY
and his neighbour says 'BILL PORLOCK, name in print,
get IN there!' while his neighbour, an elderly Irish rover
called Fergus or Angus or Mingus is muttering 'No,
I'm done with the friggin wandrin, boys...' to his done-with
    crème brulée, and Ned has seen
        all the courses come and go
        with gags and gossip to and fro
        for time is going by so slow
        it's taking you like undertow
        while at the furthest point from him
        the tall girl like a dream you dream

spoke only to some middle-aged
professor who would sometimes roar with laughter
at something he said himself and then go quiet
listening to the beauty, or glance away,
filling his glass of wine, filling her glass,
finishing off the bottle, looking around
for the out-of-work actors dressed as nymphs and shepherds
and some fool asked 'so what are you writing now?'
and his answer lasted about a bloody lifetime

    didn't it and Ned has seen

        all the courses come and go
        with jokes and joshing to and fro
        for time is going by so slow
        it's taking you like undertow
        while on the far side of the world
        the girl he'd like to be his girl

    is standing up, most people are,
the meal is over, and nothing has changed in his life
so he rips NED STOWEY to bits and then BILL PORLOCK
'I was actually going to keep that name-tag' he hears
Bill trailing him to the bar where a bearded giant
is hogging the space with his pint and living his life
'RAPHEL MAI AMECHE ZABI ALMI!' roars this ogre
to anybody in earshot and nobody knows
what in the world that means, or who he is,

    but who will ask? and Ned has seen

        all the courses come and go
        with facts and fictions to and fro
        for time is going by so slow
        time is going by so slow

it's taking you like undertow
like yesterday so long ago
today tomorrow long ago
now all the dazzled strangers make
a demi-circle round a cake
beside a little boating lake
   and in some far-off galaxy
      the girl whose boy he'd love to be
         is offering Marlboro Lights to *me!*
           I make-believe I light gladly
           in heaven
             in my own countree.

       *

'I think our professor's rat-arsed,' Mimi opines
at Ollie's side and 'I wish *I* were,' goes he.
'They stuck me between these terrible old pains
at lunch, what were they thinking?' 'Who is *they*?'

Ollie observes her lips, is about to think
he's in no mood for their shtick, when he realises
he absolutely is. 'Shall we get a drink?'
and catches her mad black moony blinking eyes

as they caught his and by that time the marquee
was where they were. 'Do you know the bride or the groom?'
goes Ollie to Mimi, then Mimi to Ollie: 'Me?
Don't know a soul, *Orlando*.' 'You know who *I* am,'

as he's ordered prosecco for both. 'I most certainly do,'
says Mimi, sipping it twice, '*way* more than you.'

*

> *You like games, O Wayne, and riddles,*
> *Guess who we three are.*

You're three sisters. Those Three Sisters. You're the Witches. You're the Corrs.

> *You like games, O Wayne, and riddles,*
> *Guess who we three are.*

The Cusacks, no the Brontes, you've a drunken brother somewhere.

> *You like games, O Wayne, and riddles,*
> *Guess who we three are.*

*

Professor	And what's your name again?
Porlock	I'm Bill Porlock.
Professor	Mm-hm, and what can I do for you.
Porlock	I'm collecting "poems" by people and apparently there are several "poets" who write "poems" here.
Professor	Yes. And?
Porlock	And I saw you sitting alone and I thought I might just seize the day. As they say.
Professor	My cup spills over.
Porlock	Hm, if you wouldn't mind speaking into this microphone.
Professor	What microphone.
Porlock	It's extremely tiny, Professor, it's cutting edge.
Professor	Is it really.
Porlock	But it *is* there.

Professor	Mm-hm. What shall I say.
Porlock	Perhaps a "poem".
	A "poem" you've written.
Professor	A "poem" I've written. Okay.
	Hang on. Gone blank. No: wait.
Porlock	Take your time, Professor.
Professor	I'll have a drink, Mr –
Porlock	Porlock.
Professor	I'll have a drink.
	Right. Here we go. Is it on?
Porlock	It's been on all the time,
	Professor.
Professor	Has it really. How can you tell.
Porlock	I'm an old hand. On the count of three. Three.
Professor	In the age of pen and paper
	When the page was a snow village
	And the light on the snow – no.
	In the age of pen and paper
	When the page was a snow village
	And the light that – the light did what...
	I'm terribly sorry but I've forgotten my own poem.
	Never mind. But I am impressed with this microphone,
	Mr –
Porlock	Porlock. Bill. Don't panic, you're not the first one.
	That man with the beard over there, he couldn't remember.
Professor	Couldn't remember what?
Porlock	He couldn't remember.
Professor	Where's Isabella? She was just here.
Porlock	Professor,

it's been a pleasure to meet.

Professor   Where's Isabella...

*

You're the Furies.

> *No, wrong./We are,*
>
> *he got it finally!/Yay.*

You're not.

> *Yes we are./No we're not, Chloe./*
>
> *We're bridesmaids: I'm Clare Tray.*

When did you make those costumes.

> *We didn't./Jen did./*
>
> *Yesterday.*

Will you have a dance with me later?

> *No./No./*
>
> *Yes if you're gay.*

*

Poet   Because I could not stop for Death –

He kindly stopped for me –

Porlock   Sorry it's a bit noisy here, love, they're moving them

tables look. Let's go round here, that's better, that's cosy.

Go again. Count of three. Three.'

Poet   Because I could not stop for Death –

He kindly stopped for me –

The Carriage held but just Ourselves –

Porlock   Sorry love, just checking, are you meaning to leave them

pauses you leave, cos I'm worried how much battery I

got left. You do? That's cool. Go on then, count of three,

three...

TIME

*

If I had all the time I had
When I arrived, when I was glad,
And I was glad when first I saw
Your face across the grassy floor –
'What's your name again?' 'Ned Stowey,
Edmund Stowey, you were on my table.'
'Really?' 'Can I go on?' 'It's a free countree.'

I glimpsed you clad in dress of green
It might as well of been a dream
And time was going faster than
It ever has, for any man,
But you and I –
'Or woman?' 'Yes, but I mean mankind.'
'Yes and womankind.' 'Yes all right all right.'
'Go on then, make those changes please.' 'Yep...'

And time was going faster than
It ever has, for any man
(Or woman) but you and I had said no word
And that to me did seem absurd.
'That line felt a bit long.' 'You made me change it.'
'Look, they're moving the tables, there'll be dancing!'
'It's just a poem...' 'Oh I'm sorry, go on, Mr Stowey.'

It seemed absurd to me that we
Were not acquainted, me and thee,
Because if time was endless I
Would bide my time and by and by
Perhaps we'd meet. But at my back
I hear Time going clickety-clack –

163

'Stop, stop, stop.' 'But this is the best part,
this is the part – ' 'I know which part it is,
Mr Stowey, it's when you ask me to make your time
nice for you. How does time go clickety-clack?
Time doesn't go clickety-clack.' 'I go on to say
it's in a cart and the *cart* goes clickety-clack.'
'It's not in a cart, Mr Stowey, it's in a sports car,
speaking of which...' 'Who's that? *He* wasn't invited!'

Bella Bella Bellissima Bella Bella fancy meeting you here... 'He's
a gatecrasher, call security! (Bollocks bollocks)'

O Bella, Bella, did anyone ever tell you that you walk in beauty
like the night of cloudless climes and starry skies, for example,
or all that's best of dark and bright pretty much meets in your
aspect and your eyes? D'ye not think so?
'No, but I was just telling Mr Stowey – Mr Stowey? That's
funny. This guy was here but he's gone.'
That's not funny remotely. It's Magnificent, Bella. You know
what, I know a much better wedding than this one…

*

They watch their old professor but he's not old,
but he sits alone and nobody thinks he's young.
From the back he looks like there's nothing he doesn't know.
Then he turns and beams at you like Santa's been.

His empty book that looks like it cost the earth
cost nothing, it was a parting gift from someone.

And it isn't empty now! He could have left
the party to scribble that which he's now writing

but he sat at the edge of the great isosceles glow
that spilled from a roaring bar at that brilliant do
to be seen as he was, neither old nor young, neither here
nor gone, neither with who he's with now, nor alone

as he is now, writing down how it was that time
there never was, when his students found this poem called

The Byelaws

Never have met me, know me well,
tell all the world there was little to tell,
say I was heavenly, say I was hell,
harry me over the blasted moors
    but come my way, go yours.

Never have touched me, take me apart,
trundle me through my town in a cart,
figure me out with the aid of a chart,
finally add to the feeble applause
    and come my way, go yours.

Never have read me, look at me now,
get why I'm doing it, don't get how,
other way round, have a rest, have a row,
have skirmishes with me, have wars,
   O come my way, go yours.

Never have left me, never come back,
mourn me in miniskirts, date me in black,
undress as I dress, when I unpack pack
yet pause for eternity on all fours
   to come my way, go yours.

Never have met me, never do,
never be mine, never even be you,
approach from a point it's impossible to
at a time you don't have, and by these byelaws
   come my way, go yours.

     *

Ed Heffenden-Dedley, SE23,
wanted the dance they would dance to be
by Abba, Adele, maybe even Jay-Z

yet Mrs Jane Angela H-D, *née*
Fackenham-Tray (Cheltenham, Chelsea, L.A.)
favours her faves at the end of the day,

dream being dream in the glitterball-glow
so round in a ring everybody they know
sort of wishes them well, sort of wishes they'd go.

*

'You could always call me Ollie, you know.' 'I could,
but where would that leave *Orlando*? Why should I care
about an Ollie, I know an *Orlando*.' 'You're mad,
you are, we're the selfsame person!' 'The hell you are.'

'Do you think they had dancing lessons, the bride and groom?'
'Not obviously.' 'Well I mean, what's *Mimi* short for?'
'It's short for me.' 'I mean what's your real name?'
'I'm not a real person, am I. Ask the author.'

'Ha! Good one. Postmodern. Wayne would approve.
Where is he.' 'Dancing. Bell's been gone a while.'
'I forgot about Bella. Completely. Cor.' 'Smart move.
Has anyone ever told you you frown when you smile?'

'Frown when I smile?' 'You did it again. You never
only smile.' 'Well, Mimi, has anyone ever
told you your lips are painted black?' 'Fuck it shows?'
'What if you needed to kiss?' 'Orlando, *lord* knows...'

*

There was a young Suitor named Stowey
Who danced with a Fury called Chloe
     To 'Brown-Eyed Girl',
     'What a Wonderful World',
Then a medley of mid-career Bowie.

*

William Jonathan Porlock
Dressed as a black-and-silver warlock

Glimpsed in the mud on the last night of Reading,
Hasn't set eyes on his mate since that wedding.

*

'Went to the woods boys I was all, I was burnin up I was,
went fishin nothing like fishin for the cool head, you know?'
'That's nice. We're off now, mister, our cab's here.' 'And, you
know, I got a, what did I get, I got a trout I did. I did!' 'Did
you.' 'I did that. Then there she was.' 'Eh? Who was?' '*She*
was, to the life.' 'Come off it. In the middle of the night, in
a wood? You don't mean the same girl, mate.' 'Eh? Same girl.
In my kitchen she was.' 'But she'd have been like eighty or
something.' 'Same girl. To the life.' 'Ri-ight. In your kitchen.
Result.' 'Said my name, she did.' 'What – Fergus?' 'Said my
fuckin *name, my name!*' 'We have to go now, Fergus.' 'Yeah,
you do, you do, got a warm warm place to go, eh.' 'Cheers,
mate, have a nice, whatever. Bye!' '...Yeah...right...a nice...
whatever...no more friggin wandrin now. Hollow lands, hilly
lands. But I'll find out where she's gone, kiss her lips I will,
take her hands I shall. Walk in the long, *dappled* grass, yes,
dappled it will be, and I shall pluck till all the times is gone,
them silver apples of the moon, I can see you, I can see you
and them, them, them golden fuckin eaters.'

*

Do you think – my Poems – are Alive – Professor –

Yeah, great...
We could look at them like, you know, on like, a date?
Where you going now?

I'm – Going – for a Walk – to Unwind –

Want, you know, company?

        Are you – Out – of your – Mind ·

       *

      ...Farewell, farewell! But this I tell
      To thee, thou Wedding-Guest!
      He prayeth well, who loveth well
      Both man and bird and beast.

      He prayeth best, who loveth best
      All things both great and small;
      For the dear God who loveth us,
      He made and loveth all.

     *

Right. – Right then, Mariner,
Cheers for the righteous rhyme.
I better be off to the wedding-feast, I –
SHIT, IS THAT THE TIME?

Jesus it's *dark*, the stars are out
Where have I been all day?
Where did I go to? What have I missed?
The guests are going away!

In twos and fours and twos and threes
They spill into cars and drive,
And some go stumbling up the hill,
I can't just like – *arrive!*

I'll just – pretend I went there too –
It's dark, they won't know me,

It's dark but at the crest of the hill
It's – unbelievably –

It's getting light! I missed the night
The sky is rosy pink!
People are dancing any old how
One makes me drink her drink

And off she goes. And no one knows
I spent the time alone
With a tale a total stranger told
Of a long old journey home!

Off she goes, and no one knows
I spent the time alone
With a tale a total stranger told
Of a long old journey home